WALKING TIME BOMB

WALKING TIME BOMB

JOHN NOSSAL

CHP

WALKING TIME-BOMB by John Nossal
Published by Creation House Press
A Charisma Media Company
600 Rinehart Road
Lake Mary, Florida 32746
www.charismamedia.com

Unless otherwise noted, all Scripture quotations are from the King James Version of the Bible.

Scripture quotations marked NLT are from the Holy Bible, New Living Translation, copyright © 1996, 2004, 2007. Used by permission of Tyndale House Publishers, Inc., Wheaton, IL 60189. All rights reserved.

Scripture quotations marked TLB are from The Living Bible. Copyright © 1971. Used by permission of Tyndale House Publishers, Inc., Wheaton, IL 60189. All rights reserved.

Design Director: Justin Evans
Cover design by Judith McKittrick-Wright

Visit the author's website: http://www.johnnossal.com.

Library of Congress Cataloging-in-Publication Data: 2015944001
International Standard Book Number: 978-1-62998-463-6
E-book International Standard Book Number: 978-1-62998-464-3

While the author has made every effort to provide accurate telephone numbers and Internet addresses at the time of publication, neither the publisher nor the author assumes any responsibility for errors or for changes that occur after publication.

First edition

15 16 17 18 19 — 9 8 7 6 5 4 3 2 1
Printed in the United States of America

DEDICATION

This book is dedicated to my loving wife, Janet, who has endured the many hardships I've experienced. She has said often that it was worse for her in my times of crisis since the Lord carried me through these perils, but not necessarily her. I'm almost inclined to agree with her. Yet, we've grown together and she has been at my side throughout. Janet, you will always be my beautiful bride, and I love you.

Also, this book is dedicated to our three unique and outstanding children—Julie, Laura, and Peter. They're so different and have been tempered through the crucible of fire of life. We remain close and our children are best of friends. I am blessed beyond measure that each one has received Jesus as Lord and maintain a personal relationship with Him. I'm comforted knowing we'll spend eternity together.

Lastly, I'm dedicating this book to my Columbia fraternity brothers and football teammates who knew me in my formative years as an undergraduate. What did I know then? However, I came away with so many fond memories of long-lost friends from my college years. Over my lifetime I've finally discovered what is vital for successful living. This book unfolds what I've discovered. Enjoy the read.

ACKNOWLEDGMENTS

THIS BOOK WOULD not have been possible if it weren't for the critical suggestions of the "backroom writers" group I attended. Thank you to Lois Blackburn, Dabney Hedegard, Jan Grandy, and Michael Wilber for your valued input. Ironically, in 1985 I was the architect for the small private Christian school where we held our meetings.

Also, I want to thank Karen Parks and my own daughter, Laura—both teachers—who so graciously proofread my manuscript and offered their valuable suggestions.

TABLE OF CONTENTS

INTRODUCTION

Some people say God is dead while others believe that if He exists, He surely doesn't involve Himself with people. I have found that God is not only alive and well, but that He is personal and always has my back. All of us have a story to tell... This is mine.

It's easy for me to be enthusiastic about God because if it weren't for Him, I'd be dead already. I survived four major surgeries—two with cancer and two with benign tumors, which weren't so benign—along with five accidents, any one of which could have been fatal. Yet, I'm still here. Throughout this story I identify these near death experiences as "... *my harrowing experience number (1-9)*." If I were in the armed services or law enforcement I could have faced deadly situations routinely, but as an architect by profession my most dangerous activity was to avoid a paper cut.

It would be too narrow to focus only on God rescuing me from death nine times, but He also led me to other experiences for the maturing of my faith, loving my wife as Christ loves the Church, raising our three children in a Christian home, routinely providing unsolicited jobs or miracle money and comforting those grieving. God has been active in many areas of my life. I have certainly not 'arrived,' but have witnessed "... *the goodness of the Lord in the land of the living*" (Psalm 27:13). Since He has been so personal and active in my life and the lives of my wife and three children, invite Him into your life, too. If you do, get ready for the ride of your life!

> "Many are the afflictions of the righteous, but the Lord delivers him out of them all."
> —Psalm 34:19

1
HEADACHES

M Y HEAD WAS pounding; it was the spring of 1979. I had gotten head-aches in the past, sometimes even migraines with the throbbing and nausea, but now they were happening too often. I visited my family doctor and when he examined me I was the picture of good health. When I mentioned that my mom occasionally got migraines when she worked, he promptly diagnosed me with "migraine syndrome." I wasn't convinced.

Next up was my wife Janet's ear, nose, and throat doctor. Did I have a sinus problem? After the ENT doctor examined me, he, too, diagnosed me with migraine syndrome, but added those words etched in my memory, "John, you know you are getting older!" Get real. I was only 34, and to think of a life with headache after headache was inconceivable.

Eventually, the migraine syndrome proved to be a misdiagnosis because I had two headaches that were beyond migraines. They were undeniable blockbusters.

The first was at Janet's end-of-the-year school faculty party. I approached the outdoor bar to get a drink with a slight headache when that mild pounding suddenly morphed into a tightening vice-like grip with my brain nearly bursting. The pain sapped my strength, and I did well just to stand. Fortunately, after several minutes the intense pain subsided and I was able to function somewhat normally.

The second was similar. As the project architect for the Esplanade Worth Avenue in Palm Beach, I had just completed an informal inspec-tion of its major tenant, Saks Fifth Avenue. As I walked back to my office just across the street, once again, that mild headache suddenly intensified into that tightening vice-like grip with excruciating pain. I was immo-bilized standing on the northeast corner of Worth Avenue and South County Road and knew I could never cross the street without collapsing. Instead, I reached out and held onto a utility pole for support. After sev-eral minutes, the intense pain eased and I crossed the street safely. One of my co-workers watched this entire scene from his office window on the third floor.

Those two headaches were not migraines!

Ten years earlier Janet's older brother, Willard, had a brain tumor and, as a precaution, she wanted me to see a neurologist. Making an appointment for a neurologist required another physician to refer me; we could not do it ourselves. With a sense of poetic justice Janet contacted her ENT doctor's office, and one of the staff made the appointment for me.

It was late May when I first met Dr. Walter Martinez, the neurologist. He examined me and didn't discern anything unusual, although he scheduled me for a CAT scan the following week.

In between appointments was Memorial Day weekend, and Janet and I had a choice of activities. Should we drive to Raiford, Florida, to attend the monthly meeting of Christian prisoners at Union Correctional Institute, or attend the Fourth Lutheran Conference of the Holy Spirit in Orlando?

On Friday, May 25th, I had another headache and simply couldn't travel. Goodbye, Raiford! The appeal of the Lutheran conference was that the main speaker was Benny Hinn, a person reputed to have a healing ministry. Although I didn't know what was causing these headaches, I needed to be healed of something.

The next day Janet and I, along with our daughters, eight-year-old Julie and four-year-old Laura, drove to Orlando to attend the conference.

Benny Hinn spoke on Saturday evening, May 26th. He gave a dynamic message about developing the mind of Christ and actually demonstrated the power of the Holy Spirit. As a Lutheran that was an eye-opener for me. He called for all the children in the conference to line up in front of the stage and, with his arm extended, passed by each one of them. As he passed by, every child, including Julie and Laura, threw his or her arms in the air and fell backwards. Benny Hinn touched no one. That could never have been choreographed at such a spontaneous event, particularly with young children. I have since learned that Spirit-filled believers call such an experience as being "slain in the Spirit."

Benny Hinn wasn't done yet. He sensed the strong presence of the Spirit and attempted a bold thing; he wanted all the people in the auditorium to be slain in the Spirit at their seats. He requested that we all stand. I was probably 100 feet away from the stage and when I stood up, I felt a force pushing against me even though nobody was there! I just experienced a spiritual shock wave pulsating towards me with Benny Hinn at the epicenter. How could I ignore what just happened?

Something similar is recorded in the Bible at John 18:1-6. Jesus had just gone to the Garden of Gethsemane with his disciples late at night immediately before His betrayal. Judas, his betrayer, finally arrived with a detachment of troops, armed with weapons, to arrest Jesus. When Jesus asked them who they were seeking and they said Jesus of Nazareth, verse 6 records the following: "Now when He said to them, 'I am He,' they drew back and fell to the ground." Why would a detachment of troops, armed for conflict, all fall to the ground? Could they have been "slain in the Spirit?"

On Memorial Day, the moderator of the conference announced Benny Hinn's upcoming schedule; he would be speaking at a church in West Palm Beach the next two nights, Tuesday and Wednesday. Wow! That's our home turf. Was this merely a coincidence or, as one of my friends would say, a "God-incident?" Janet and I were there both nights and, once again, we saw Benny Hinn minister in a hot, crowded church and saw the effects of the Holy Spirit flowing through him. I received prayer the second night from Suzanne, Benny Hinn's fiancée, and when she laid her hands on me I felt my body burning up—like a fever, except I wasn't sick. Spiritually, I was soaring.

The very next day, Thursday, May 31st, one day before our eleventh wedding anniversary, I saw Dr. Walter Martinez and had the CAT scan. Janet was understandably nervous, but friends comforted her by saying if there was nothing seriously wrong with me, the doctor's office would likely contact us in a week or so with the results. However, if the doctor wanted to see us immediately after the scan, there would not be good news.

Dr. Martinez wanted to see us after the scan.

After playing eight years of high school and college football relatively unscathed with no broken bones or even a stitch, Dr. Martinez looked me in the eye and said with extraordinary compassion, "You have a brain tumor!"

Those words stunned me. It never occurred to me that I would have a brain tumor. Doesn't that happen to somebody else...anybody else...not to me? Yet, in a bizarre way, I was also relieved...maybe I could be healed. It would have been worse to have those excruciating headaches with no cure in sight.

At the center of this trial was God, Himself. In His mercy and grace He prepared me to receive this potentially devastating news. I had just seen Benny Hinn for the third time in a span of five days, within the last

24 hours at that, and was on the mountaintop, a spiritual high. Although stunned initially, I retained my peace and, believe it or not, experienced no fear.

Dr. Martinez even showed me the CAT scan and there was something that looked like a robin's egg growing behind my left eye in the middle of my brain. It appeared to be well-confined without tentacles spreading out, common to many tumors, and we were both optimistic it was benign. Finally, he told me the tumor would need to be removed surgically. I was about to have brain surgery.

Dr. Martinez oozed sympathy for me, for which I was grateful. How does a doctor tell somebody that his life may soon be over? Later, he told us that in his practice at that time only two or three people with headaches as their only symptom actually had brain tumors. It was extremely rare.

Janet was badly shaken, so Dr. Martinez wrote a prescription of Valium for her. However, after taking only one pill, she threw the rest away since being drugged provided no comfort. I still had the brain tumor after all. Now we had to tell family and friends.

2
SPREADING THE NEWS

ONE OF THE first people I phoned was Mom. She loves me as only a mother could, but I had to tell her that her "little Johnnie" had a brain tumor and would have imminent surgery. Being the quiet type, she was understandably pensive before asking, "Was it because of playing football?" She may have felt a twinge of guilt, but I reassured her that it wasn't and reminded her that I had worn a helmet to protect my head.

Lew and Linda Brown were friends we planned to visit that summer in Menlo Park, California. We met them ten years earlier at a young adults group at St. Andrew's Lutheran Church in Pittsburgh. Ironically, we lived on the same street in Squirrel Hill, a Jewish neighborhood, and were likely the only two Gentile couples on that block of about ten apartment buildings with over 100 units.

When we contacted Lew and Linda and told them I was just diagnosed with a brain tumor, they were naturally surprised and could not have been more sympathetic. Linda telephoned Stanford to check out their neurological department, but realized it would not suit me.

Of course, I had to tell Gene Lawrence, my boss, that I had a brain tumor and would need surgery. He confessed to me much later that he thought he would never see me again.

One of my friends from church, Kirt Danielson, offered me financial support if I needed it. Kirt was not wealthy, but he was certainly rich in empathy. Fortunately, I didn't need money.

After telephoning friends in church and those in our Christian community, we were not besieged with calls; instead, our phone became strangely silent. What do you say to a person with a brain tumor whose life span was on a short list?

If we ever tried to figure out what caused the tumor, I had several events in my childhood that were prime candidates. Kids take hard knocks while growing up, and I was no exception. My most severe knocks, however, were directed to my head, any one of which may have caused the tumor.

Dr. Martinez even said it may have been genetic...I may have been born with it.

When I was about eight years old, I was playing a game with classmates and we were running across our elementary schoolyard. Boys love to run fast, and I was racing. Unfortunately, about five feet from the school building, I tripped and slammed head-first into the brick wall. The wall never budged, but I bounced off, utterly dazed, and rolled over on my back. Every movement was in slow motion, or at least that's what my brain was telling me. A few seconds later, I regained my senses and resumed playing. I doubt if anybody even saw what happened because nobody said anything. I remain grateful my neck didn't snap.

A couple of years later on a winter day, I rode my bike to the local park to play on the frozen lake with neighborhood friends. One of my neighbors, who wasn't so friendly, thought it would be fun to run behind me, slide on the ice, and knock my feet out from under me. He was amused at my expense. The back of my skull hit the ice with a thud, like dropping a hundred twenty-pound weight from a five-foot height, and I likely had a concussion. When I rode my bike home I literally couldn't see straight; I had to turn my head to the left to see what was directly in front of me. I made it home safely, but wasn't feeling well and did the one thing doctors say to avoid: I slept.

Neither George—my older brother—nor Mom knew where I was, and she was near panic. Dad was working. Finally, she went to her bedroom and saw me sleeping in her bed. Nobody thought of looking there since I had never done that before. She was relieved when she woke me up, and I was relieved because I could see straight ahead once again. I never saw a doctor about the injury, though I still have a knot on the back of my skull where I hit the ice.

The third incident may seem funny to some, but I never laughed. I was about ten or eleven and Dad, George, and I were playing baseball in that local park, the same one with the frozen lake incident. My dad pitched, George—over 6'0" tall—hit, and I shagged the balls. Eventually, I got tired of running all over the outfield and started to jog in; I wanted to hit. I yelled to Dad and George that I was coming in, but neither heard me and continued what they were doing. Dad pitched and George hit.

The odds of what happened next are no doubt astronomical. I had my head down blithely jogging to the infield when George hit a screeching line drive. That baseball had eyes; it slammed right into my forehead.

What a shot! Dad and George immediately rushed to me, but by the time they reached me, I already had a half inch high "goose-egg" on the left side of my forehead where the ball hit me.

I've heard the bone of the forehead is the strongest of the entire body, and I needed every bit of its strength that day. If the ball were five inches higher, I never would have been hit; if it were five inches lower, who knows how many teeth would have been shattered. I never got to hit that day, but I did survive.

Also, what was the toll on my head after playing high school and college football for eight years? Even the most casual football fan realizes that players are susceptible to concussions. Although I wore a helmet to protect my head, there was one play in college in which my helmet was knocked off while the action continued. Fortunately, my opponent avoided slamming my exposed head. He was from Harvard.

However, in my sophomore year at Columbia during one of our midweek scrimmages, I was playing offensive tackle against a senior who was simply nasty. Defensive linemen are taught to use their forearm as a weapon, called a forearm shiver. The intent is to hit the offensive lineman's chest, get under him and control him. Instead, on one play Mr. Nasty purposely slammed his forearm directly into the side of my helmet. Instantly, I saw a galaxy of stars and momentarily staggered like a boxer who just took a devastating shot to the head. Fortunately, I recovered quickly and wouldn't give him the satisfaction of knowing he just knocked me silly. Although that was a severe blow to my head, it still paled in comparison to the others.

To ascertain what caused my brain tumor was irrelevant. It was vital that it be removed!

The following Wednesday, June 6, 1979, I had an appointment with a neurosurgeon referred by Dr. Walter Martinez (neurosurgeons operate, neurologists diagnose). This neurosurgeon discussed surgery options with Janet and me and made a statement I've never forgotten, *"John, right now, you're a walking time-bomb and if you would pass out and nobody were around, you would die!"* Time was not on my side.

Janet's family strongly believed that if major surgery were necessary, one should get the best surgeon available. Dr. Martinez knew I wanted a second opinion and, since I was a Columbia alumnus, he contacted the Neurological Institute at the Presbyterian Hospital in the City of New York, Columbia's medical school. He made an appointment for me with a leading neurosurgeon, who I'll call Dr. McFarland, for June 12, 1979, at 1:00 PM and even arranged to have me admitted the next day for brain surgery.

I mention 1:00 PM because Janet and I made a second appointment that same day with another neurosurgeon in Boston at 4:00 PM. Linda Brown, during her inquiries at Stanford, learned of a world-renowned neurosurgeon who practiced at a Boston hopsital. Because Linda went to such efforts to find such a renowned neurosurgeon and my brother, George, happened to live just outside Boston, we made that second appointment for June 12th.

I knew with brain surgery I might die. Others faced "life or death" situations, so how would I handle mine? I was on the proverbial mountaintop after seeing Benny Hinn and even after being told of my brain tumor, I had peace. After a week, however, I needed to replenish that peace and reading the Bible boosted my spirit. The scripture that comforted me most was 2 Corinthians 5:8 when Paul wrote: *"... to be absent from the body and to be present with the Lord."* Simply put, if I were to die, I would be with Jesus and to me that was *really* good news. All of us will die eventually unless the rapture happens in our lifetime (1 Thessalonians 4:16–17)—that is, the supernatural removal of Christians from planet Earth—but my overriding concern was where I would spend eternity? The thought of being with Jesus comforted me.

Also, I realized that people having brain surgery might suffer permanent physical disabilities. That thought was more difficult to accept, but again, I meditated on the scripture describing the Apostle Paul's *"thorn in the flesh"* (2 Corinthians 12:7–9). He prayed to the Lord three times to remove it, but instead of removing it the Lord answered Paul by saying, *"My grace is sufficient for you, for My strength is made perfect in weakness."* I reasoned that if the Lord's grace were sufficient for Paul, then, somehow, His grace would sustain me also. That, too, comforted me.

Unfortunately, Janet did not share my positive outlook. She maintained that my brain tumor was actually harder on the loved ones because the Lord "carried" me through this perilous path, but not her. She's probably right as she was tortured emotionally throughout this ordeal; however, I experienced peace and had no fear, which, in human terms, is simply not normal. Yet, it was the Lord who directed me to Benny Hinn for just that purpose.

On Friday, June 8th, Janet and I were expecting a quiet evening at home, but the Lord had a different plan. Friends of ours from Cursillo (a Christian leaders' weekend), two couples from Boca Raton, drove up to surprise us. Then, Jim—my friend from church—and his wife also dropped in for a visit. Finally, a dear Christian brother who was part of my weekly group-reunion showed up. Completely unplanned, seven of our closest friends visited us that evening to pray for me and celebrate life...we had a party!

Our daughters, Julie and Laura, were eight and four respectively. Laura was too young to understand what was happening to me, but Julie wasn't. Before traveling north, Janet knew she must tell Julie about my critical condition was because if I were to die and Julie were uninformed, she may never forgive her mom. How it happened was not planned. While Janet drove Julie to a ballet lesson, Julie sensed the seriousness of my surgery and actually asked her mom if I were about to die. Tough question. Janet considered her answer before finally answering by saying, "I don't know."

3
THE PLAN

WE ARRANGED TO have our two young daughters spend the next month or so with Janet's parents in Pittsburgh while I convalesced at my childhood home in Connecticut. Monday, June 11th, was travel day. We put Julie and Laura on a flight from Palm Beach International to Pittsburgh and, understandably, it was a tearful departure. Our daughters had never traveled alone before and, although unspoken, we all realized they might never see me again. After our girls took off, Janet and I patiently waited for our early afternoon flight to New York City. After a brief delay, it was routine.

Although my parents lived in Connecticut, a little more than an hour to the airport, my dad avoided that drive because of the potential traffic congestion. Instead, Janet and I would use a limousine service to transport us from the airport to my home town of Bridgeport.

After landing we exited the plane, called for a limousine and were impressed when it arrived so quickly. Sadly, our luggage never got off the plane. Naturally, we were unhappy as we watched that limousine disappear, but had to wait for our luggage. Finally, we retrieved our suitcases and phoned for another limousine.

Traffic around the New York airports in late afternoon becomes gridlocked, and it was now late afternoon. What should have taken a little more than one hour wound up taking nearly three hours. I was irritated at the stop-and-go traffic and during that crowded limousine ride spoke to no one except Janet. I clutched my briefcase containing that precious CAT scan for the two appointments the next day.

At Fairfield, Connecticut, the last stop before Bridgeport, everybody exited the limousine except one other passenger, the driver, Janet and me. For whatever reason, that other passenger turned around and cheerfully asked, "What are you guys doing in New York…on a vacation?" In no mood to mince words, I told him bluntly: "No, I'm here to have brain surgery." However, I quickly added that we were Christians and believed that everything would turn out well. After telling him that we were interviewing two neurosurgeons the next day, he said that he, too, was a Christian and wanted to help.

He introduced himself as "Peter" and told us he lived in Middletown, Connecticut, where he knew a retired neurosurgeon. He asked me for the names of the two neurosurgeons I would be interviewing the next day and when he arrived home would telephone his retired friend and inquire about my doctors. That sounded reasonable to me so I wrote down the names of the two neurosurgeons along with my parent's phone number just as we pulled into the Bridgeport limousine stop. My parents were waiting for us and we drove home where my mom, who is such a great cook, made chicken noodle soup with homemade noodles. Doesn't that cure everything?

As soon as we finished eating, the telephone rang and it was Peter from the limousine. He was very excited because he just telephoned his retired neurosurgeon friend and inquired about the two doctors I would see the next day. *The retired neurosurgeon said that he was their professor in medical school and they were two of his best students.*

Whoa! What are the chances of meeting a stranger in a limousine who just happened to know a retired neurosurgeon who just happened to be the professor of the two doctors I would see the very next day and they were two of his best students? Was this merely another "coincidence?" Maybe, just maybe, the Lord *was* leading me. Proverbs 16:9 says, *"A man's heart plans his way, but the Lord directs his steps."*

What a tremendous boost that gave Janet and me. By faith, I traveled up north to have brain surgery, but didn't know who would do it, where it would be or when it would be done...a few loose ends there! And I was the *walking time-bomb*. With that affirmation from Peter, I experienced *"the goodness of the Lord in the land of the living."* (Psalm 27:13).

On Tuesday, June 12th, Janet and I took the train from Bridgeport to New York City for our appointment with Dr. McFarland. Since I made that trip countless times as a college student, it was not difficult to take the shuttle from Grand Central Station to Times Square and then take the IRT subway to Broadway and West 168th Street to the Neurological Institute. We arrived at our appointment early, rare for me, and as we waited, a bald man in a white gown approached us. We didn't know if he was a patient or doctor, but it was Dr. McFarland. He, too, arrived early.

Our appointment with Dr. McFarland was perfect. After reviewing my CAT scan, he described to us how he would perform surgery. He would cut my scalp from ear to ear over the top of my skull so that the scar would be concealed by my hair, pull the skin back (which he affectionately called a "scalping") and perform a craniotomy by removing a portion of the left frontal section of my skull and go straight down through my brain to remove the tumor.

Strangely enough, his description comforted me. I had heard that separating the hemispheres and going down through the middle of the brain might cause memory damage since memory is stored at that intersection. He was also very upbeat about the prognosis, but, of course, couldn't guarantee the tumor would be benign until a biopsy was performed. Nevertheless, Dr. McFarland's positive attitude encouraged us.

Finally, with the appointment over, Janet told Dr. McFarland that we were Christians and believed in the power of prayer. Dr. McFarland smiled broadly and told us that as a young man he had a career choice to make— to become either a Presbyterian minister or a neurosurgeon. He chose to become a neurosurgeon, but prayed for each one of his patients prior to surgery.

Janet then told him of our plans to interview his colleague and classmate at 4:00 PM that same afternoon in Boston. As we were leaving he told us to say "hi" to his classmate. We left Dr. McFarland's office comforted, pleased and early.

It was good to be early since we planned to take a taxi to Kennedy Airport and board a shuttle flight from New York to Boston. George would meet us at the airport and drive us to my appointment at the Boston hospital. Our taxi made such good time to the airport that we actually booked an earlier shuttle flight. The flight was short, and before we knew it we were descending into Boston, an hour earlier than expected.

Immediately after exiting the shuttle, we were standing in that enormous waiting room at Logan International Airport when I said to Janet, "Where can we wait, so that we won't miss George?" I no sooner spoke those words when George appeared coming up the escalator less than 30 feet away. When I asked him why he arrived so early he replied rather flippantly, "I just felt like it."

As George drove us to my second appointment, I realized that monumental decision before me. How could I decide who would do surgery? My appointment with Dr. McFarland was perfect and, because of the efforts by Dr. Martinez, I was already checked into Columbia Presbyterian Hospital the following day. But I hadn't even met the world-famous neurosurgeon in Boston. So I offered a simple prayer that the Lord would show me who would be my surgeon; I couldn't make that decision alone.

Once again, we arrived early for my scheduled 4:00 PM appointment. Unfortunately, this doctor was nearly one hour late. As positive and upbeat as Dr. McFarland was, his classmate stressed the negative. He told me about the possibilities of dying, malignancy, chemotherapy, radiation or being permanently disabled. And then, he delivered the "Coup de Grace." *He couldn't take me because his schedule was full.*

My prayer about who would perform surgery was just answered rather emphatically. Ironically, hanging on the wall of this doctor's office was a watercolor painted by the retired neurosurgeon from Middletown, Connecticut, who the day before spoke those beautiful words of encouragement. What a priceless experience.

After the appointment, George drove Janet and me from Boston to Bridgeport, but had to return home that same evening. He was always such a good big brother and really helped me that day.

Wednesday would be check-in day into Columbia's medical school for brain surgery, hardly the jubilant college homecoming I envisioned.

4
SURGERY

O<small>N</small> W<small>EDNESDAY</small>, D<small>AD</small>, Mom, and Janet drove me to the Neurological Institute for Friday's surgery. It was an older building, and when we walked into my room overlooking the Hudson River, what struck me was the little fan on the wall—that was my air conditioning. The nurses assured me, however, that the important rooms, such as surgical suites, were air-conditioned. Fortunately, the weather was pleasant in New York that spring.

When my folks and Janet left that day, I sensed their melancholy, since there were no guarantees I would survive brain surgery. Because of a gasoline shortage, Dad was not returning until Friday. Janet was distraught knowing she couldn't be with me one final day; instead, she remained with her in-laws, hardly the comfort she sought. Yet, I had peace and never envisioned Janet becoming a widow at such an early age, merely three days before her thirty-third birthday. As God the Holy Spirit continued to sustain me, He would also have to comfort Janet, Mom, and Dad; that's one of His roles.

After suffering through headache after headache that spring, including those two blockbusters, something unexpected happened. I had experienced no headaches for the past three weeks and felt well. My last headache was on Friday, May 25th, and I became curious as to whether or not the brain tumor even remained. My thinking may have seemed odd, but I witnessed and even experienced the sheer power of the Holy Spirit in a Benny Hinn service three times and was covered with prayers from so many people that God may have already zapped it with His laser.

Dr. McFarland answered that one, however, when he ordered a CAT scan on Thursday, June 14th to confirm the position of the tumor and, sure enough, it was still there.

Also, on that Thursday, I wrote down the events of the past several weeks, filling six pages from my legal pad. There was no guarantee my memory would be intact after surgery and I never wanted to forget the past three weeks, highlighted by Peter from the limousine.

I did have a surprise visitor, a Lutheran minister. Apparently, my former pastor from Florida, now a bishop, contacted people in New York and arranged for this visit… perhaps the Lutheran version of the last rites. Although the minister prayed for me, a person who might not be alive after brain surgery the next day, I sensed his awkwardness. I believe my peace ministered to him more than he ministered to me. Still, I was grateful for his visit and the concern of my former pastor and friend.

As expected, later that afternoon, the hospital staff shaved my head in preparation for surgery. What I didn't expect is that the staff saved my hair in a paper bag. Apparently, there was a New York state law that mandated that if I expired, a hairpiece could be made using my own hair. Had I known that, I would have shampooed my hair first.

I don't remember much about the day of surgery, Friday, June 15th. I was so relaxed that when given some Demoral very early in the morning before the anesthesia, I conked out. I was told that it was a long surgery, about thirteen hours, and that it went well.

Dr. McFarland and his surgical team performed the surgery and removed the tumor that was encapsulated in the left ventricle behind my left eye in the middle of my brain. Because he was so confident of completely removing it, I had no radiation or chemotherapy. After surgery, I was left with a couple of pronounced dimples in my skull, collateral damage of that craniotomy, which is a constant reminder of brain surgery.

With the tumor located in the ventricle, the spinal fluid was impeded from circulating through my brain normally, which had caused those headaches. With the tumor removed, I experienced no more headaches.

The biopsy identified the tumor as a benign astrocytoma—a particularly virulent tumor. Coincidentally, there was a Reader's Digest article circulating at the same time about another brain tumor patient who had an astrocytoma. That tumor was given the nicknamed "killer" for the obvious reason that it killed people.

But I lived! I was bathed in prayer from my Christian community which included my family, church friends, the Cursillo community in South Florida, the prisoners at the Union Correctional Institute who were just beginning UCI Cursillo #5 on the morning of June 15th, and a dear Christian friend who had just begun working for *The 700 Club* in Virginia Beach and had put me on their prayer list.

Janet, meanwhile, was emotionally unnerved, but patiently waited for Dad to drive to the hospital. Knowing that surgery would likely be an all-day affair, they arrived late that morning. Before parking the car, my parents dropped off Janet at the hospital entrance and she bolted for the front door rushing to my room for any news about surgery.

Janet got on the elevator and it was crowded. People on crowded elevators usually don't talk, particularly at a hospital for brain surgery, but a doctor in the elevator asked Janet, "Who are you visiting?" Janet was teary-eyed, but managed to say, "My husband, he's having brain surgery." It was quiet in the elevator before this, but now there was absolute silence. The doctor continued, "What's his name?" She replied, "John Nossal." Amazingly, he said, "Oh! I was just with him and he's doing fine."

At a teaching hospital, one of the ways a doctor learns is by observation and this doctor was observing my surgery and just happened to be taking the same elevator at the same time as Janet. We found out later that a friend of ours from Cursillo, a nurse herself, had this rather thoughtful prayer, "Please send an angel (messenger) to Janet to comfort her during John's surgery." We believe the doctor was that "angel" sent to comfort her.

When Janet exited the elevator, she went to my room and saw my handwritten account and the paper bag. Opening the bag, she saw my hair, not the best thing to see during surgery, especially when she asked why the hair was saved and the staff told her of the New York state law. That little tidbit of information offered her no comfort.

Janet and my parents then waited, and waited, and waited. Finally, about 7:30 PM Dr. McFarland arrived. He saw Janet first, who was pacing the hallway outside my room, and told her that he removed the tumor and I was alive and well, although sedated, and was recovering in the intensive care unit (ICU). With so much pent-up emotion, Janet immediately burst into tears and made her way into the room where my parents were patiently waiting. Seeing Janet crying, they thought I had died! Janet quickly assured them that I was alive and, by this time, Dr. McFarland joined them and gave them a brief account of surgery and how well I did.

Dr. McFarland's words comforted my family and after he left, the three of them held hands in the room and thanked God I had just survived brain surgery. Since I was still unconscious, they couldn't see me that night, but all returned home relieved.

5
POST-OP

I WOKE UP EARLY Saturday morning in the ICU. Any recovery in an ICU is serious because of the nature of the surgeries. In the Neurological Institute this was especially true as one of the other patients in that same ICU did pass away. We heard his loved ones grieving.

However, I felt surprisingly well. I wasn't about to play tennis, but was lucid, bored, and with nothing to do, the staff did for me something that was rare. They wheeled in a television set into my little cubicle so I could watch America's favorite pastime—baseball.

Later in the day, Janet and my parents arrived. Since they couldn't all fit into my ICU unit at the same time, Janet entered first. When she saw me sitting up in bed with my head wrapped in bandages with a tube draining excess fluids from my skull watching a baseball game, she gasped. That was not how she expected to see me the day after surgery. She was overjoyed until I asked her to phone Gene Lawrence in Florida, just to tell him I survived. She became flustered and couldn't remember the number, and, without thinking, I blurted out his full telephone number, area code and all. At that point I was overjoyed because my memory was working.

Dr. McFarland cautioned Janet and my folks that my brain may have to "rearrange" itself and that they shouldn't be alarmed at what I may say. What did that mean? We found out several days later.

My parents were with me in my hospital room when I announced, "When I return to Florida, have FPL remove my brain tumor." (FPL is Florida Power & Light, our local electric utility.) My dad was stunned, but trying to remain as cool as possible, he immediately left the room, sought out Janet and told her what I just said. Together, they came into the room and with my dad gripping the side rails of my bed with knuckles white, Janet asked me to repeat what I just said. So I repeated it, "When I return to Florida, have FPL remove my brain tumor."

Now, they all scrambled to find Dr. McFarland. He came into my room smiling and calmly asked me to repeat what I had just told my family. "When I return to Florida, have FPL remove my brain tumor." He looked at me and asked, "John, does that make sense?" I said "no" and he then reassured Janet and my parents that everything would be fine. I had come so far and recovered so well that I unnerved my family with those words. Fortunately, that was the only time that my brain had to "rearrange" itself.

I was released from the hospital on Saturday, June 23rd, and my family drove me home to convalesce. My mom had given us her bedroom, and Janet was so delighted to finally be alone with me that on the first night, she seduced me. I never complained, but much later, when we saw Dr. McFarland and we told him what we did, he said that was a no-no because the excitement could have killed me. Apparently, we just affirmed that cliché, "Ignorance is bliss."

For the next year after surgery, I needed to take an anti-seizure drug and the doctor prescribed Dilantin. After a week at my parent's home, I woke up agitated and Janet asked me what was wrong. "I itch!" Apparently, I was allergic to Dilantin. Immediately, we called Dr. McFarland's office and he prescribed another drug called Myselene, but, sadly, I was allergic to that one also. Finally, Dr. McFarland prescribed the good, old faithful, Phenobarbital. (Janet's brother, Will, had taken Phenobarbital after his brain surgery and it slows everything down.) Bingo! I wasn't allergic to Phenobarbital and took it faithfully for one year. I never had a seizure.

After a month of convalescing in Connecticut, I was ready to return to Florida. Julie and Laura re-joined us in Bridgeport and we almost didn't recognize them since each one gained nearly ten pounds. We never considered the stress my surgery would impose on Janet's mom who literally gave our daughters their own food cart in the supermarket. It showed.

When we took our flight home to West Palm Beach, we were greeted by about a dozen friends from church, some holding signs of greeting and get-well messages. I felt like a celebrity. People from our Christian community mowed our lawn, maintained our swimming pool and even stocked our refrigerator for our homecoming. We were blessed with so much love, care and prayers.

Within weeks of returning, I began working full time as an architect and a rather unique experience was behind me. For the next five years I had CAT scans to detect any unusual brain activity, but remained tumor free and healthy.

Quoted below is a contemporary Christian parable called "Footprints":

One night a man had a dream. He dreamed
he was walking along the beach with the Lord.

Across the sky flashed scenes from his life.
For each scene he noticed two sets of
footprints in the sand; one belonging
to him and the other to the Lord.

When the last scene of his life flashed before
him, he looked back at the footprints in the
sand. He noticed that many times along the
path of his life there was only *one* set of footprints.

He also noticed that it happened at the very
lowest and saddest times of his life.
This really bothered him and he
questioned the Lord about it.

"Lord, you said that once I decided to follow
you, you'd walk with me all the way.
But I have noticed that during the most
troublesome times in my life,
there was only one set of footprints.
I don't understand why when
I needed you most you would leave me."

The Lord replied:
"My son, my precious child,
I love you and would never leave you.
During the times of trial and suffering,
when you see only one set of footprints,
it was then that I carried you."

I had just lived that parable. *This concludes my "harrowing experience Number Two"!* (Number One occurred twelve years earlier.)

6
THE BEGINNING

MY STORY ACTUALLY began 13 years earlier, on June 1, 1966, with commencement exercises from Columbia University. It was such an honor to put on my cap and gown after spending four years of studying hard, as well as having so much fun. My friends on the football team and fraternity brothers certainly enriched my entire college experience and my only regret was that I'd miss my days as an undergraduate, never to be repeated. But life moves on and now it was my turn.

After graduation my parents and two favorite uncles—Uncle Paul and Uncle John from New Kensington, Pennsylvania (near Pittsburgh), drove me to Times Square for an Italian feast at Mama Leone's. While we celebrated quietly, I privately savored the task just completed. Afterward, my parents and uncles left for home while I returned to campus to continue celebrating.

Unlike the time spent with family, my college friends and I were boisterous to a fault. I didn't get much sleep that night, but then again, how often does one graduate from college?

I had the good fortune to be accepted into the architectural program at Carnegie Institute of Technology in Pittsburgh, later renamed Carnegie-Mellon University. One of the reasons for applying to Carnegie Tech was that if I ever became homesick, I could always visit my relatives in New Kensington. Not surprisingly, I never became homesick.

The following morning I took a train from Grand Central Station to Bridgeport, Connecticut, and spent the day with family.

However, the war drums were beating louder in a place called Vietnam and in order to secure a student deferment, I needed to pass a draft deferment test given on Columbia's campus the very next day, June 3rd. In the early evening I returned to New York City by train. Before leaving, Uncle Paul gave me sage advice by telling me to get a good eight hours sleep before the test. Although I loved my uncle, I ignored his advice.

What I never told my family is that I had a date with Annie, a coed I'd met recently. It was a late date and I didn't get much sleep that night either. What was I thinking? I was about to take a test to determine where I would spend my immediate future, either as a student at Carnegie Tech or possibly as an army draftee in Vietnam fighting a war, and I'm the one who had no more than four hours sleep for not one, but two nights in a row. What *was* I thinking?

The morning of the test did not start out well for me. Taking a shower usually revived me, but not that time. I may have been clean, but remained utterly exhausted.

The test itself wasn't particularly difficult, a multiple choice exam, and under normal circumstances, I would have breezed through it. But the lack of sleep really caught up to me and my brain was processing those questions in sluggish mode at best. I deluded myself into thinking I was doing well, but that ended abruptly when the proctor announced there was one minute remaining. Oh no! There were still *eleven* questions left with no time to even read them let alone determine correct answers. With my mind in super slow motion, I made a lightening fast decision. I marked the answer "B" for the last eleven questions hoping that I would at least get a couple right. I certainly didn't finish the test with a flourish, but was relieved it was over.

After the test I met my parents and uncles on campus and together we began our car trip to New Kensington for a family vacation. Needless to say, I slept in the car.

In order to obtain a student deferment the government required that undergraduates score at least a 70 and graduate students an 80 on the test. I was a graduate student; my score was an 81! *Somebody* was surely watching over me.

That September I left for Pittsburgh to continue my education as an architectural student at Carnegie Tech. My roommate was Gary from San Diego who was enrolled in the MBA program and we roomed together in the graduate dorm. We got along quite well and he was the person who taught me to play bridge, which I enjoy to this day. I vividly remember our first-year architectural design instructor telling the incoming students that if we were going into architecture for the money, don't. I didn't believe him.

After completing my first year at Carnegie Tech, I returned to Bridgeport for my summer vacation and began working for West End Moving & Storage, a local moving company. I needed money. Fortunately, I had my football-playing physique—6'2", 210 pounds and strong. Nevertheless, life throws some curveballs along the way and I've always had trouble hitting curves.

One day, I was assigned the task of an office move, which consisted of relocating one Xerox business machine on the second floor. Xerox business machines in 1967 were *large and heavy*. It was too big to fit on the elevator and the only way to move it out of the building was to carry it down a very wide stairway leading to the front door. The floor-to-floor height was about eighteen feet.

There were three of us assigned to this task: Lenny, the driver, who was thin, but strong, Frank, a very stocky man—built-like-bull—and me. The plan was that I would be on the bottom carrying the machine while descending backward on the stairs, Lenny would be behind me supporting my back, while Frank would be above holding the machine with a very heavy duty strap.

As we began our descent, because of the angle of the stairway, I had my neck pressed against the side of the machine. Did I know what I was doing? How could I? I was a rookie. After only a couple of steps downward with my neck pressing against steel, my carotid artery was compressed and WHAM...*I passed out and dropped like a rock!*

Lenny and Frank immediately sprang into crisis mode. Lenny stiff-armed the machine from the bottom while Frank pulled back on that heavy duty strap with all his strength. My limp 210-pound body could have been crushed by that steel-framed, Xerox monster hovering above me with gravity pulling it down. Miraculously, they managed to keep it from tumbling over me.

Within a minute I regained consciousness, stood up on the stairway and, without saying a word, took the bottom right corner of the machine, while Lenny took the bottom left corner. With Frank still holding onto that strap for dear life, we managed to carry it safely down the stairway to the first floor.

Not only was disaster averted, as that Xerox machine would have been destroyed, causing damage to the building and likely injuring both Lenny and Frank, but I would have been crushed like a bug. Immediately, I realized I was fortunate to be alive. We didn't talk about the "what-ifs" that day, but I was one thankful person knowing that, once again, *Somebody* was watching over me. I had just survived my *"harrowing experience number one!"*

7
ROMANCE AND WEDDING BELLS

M Y YEARS AT Carnegie-Mellon were highlighted by an event on June 1, 1968, exactly two years after graduating from Columbia. I got married.

My relationship with Janet was certainly not "love at first sight," since she had first dated my roommate, Gary, and I had actually double-dated with Gary and Janet on several occasions. Strangely enough, *I never noticed her.* To me Janet was always "Gary's date," which meant hands off. That changed abruptly on a Wednesday afternoon in the fall of 1967, when Janet, who loves movies, wanted a ride to see a ladies' day matinee…Elizabeth Taylor and Richard Burton in *Night of the Iguana.* She went to the student union, and I happened to be the only guy there she knew with a car, so she impulsively asked me if I would take her to the movie. *Where's Gary?* I wondered. I had to cut an architectural design class that afternoon to become Janet's chauffeur.

We saw the movie, I got a parking ticket, and Gary was upset. He phoned Janet that evening and confronted her by asking "What were you doing dating my roommate?" Janet's response: "That wasn't a date!" In her mind she simply needed a ride and I had a car.

Two days later, however, while visiting a local pub, I ran into Janet, who was mildly inebriated, and she asked me when I would finally take her out on a real date. I got the hint, and she never asked again. Within a matter of weeks, it seemed as though scales fell from my eyes and I saw her for the first time. I fell hard and wanted her for my bride.

We were both Protestant, college-educated, had good families and our personalities were total opposites, which I found magnetic. If I were ever asked to describe my "ideal woman," she would be tall, blonde with blue eyes, well-endowed, long-legged, shapely, and attractive. Her name was Janet. She liked the fact that I would become an architect, likely make a ton of money and envisioned her life as a stay-at-home mom raising a family; she wanted babies. We were both primed for surprises.

I've heard that many couples have a memory of "The Kiss" and we have

23

ours. At a party a couple weeks after we had started dating, I was sitting in a chair with Janet curled up on the floor in front of me. I leaned over her, tilted her head toward me, and kissed her tenderly on the lips for a long time. Wow! We were both smitten.

Not everything was smooth sailing, however.

After another party one of Janet's girlfriends asked her how she enjoyed the party and she replied, "How could you have a good time if you're with somebody you can't stand?" The very next week Janet saw the same girlfriend and told her that she was getting married. To whom? To me, the same guy she said she couldn't stand the week before. I was riding one emotional roller coaster.

Being proper, I needed to ask Janet's dad for permission to marry his daughter and how it happened was significant, at least to me. In the late '60s, college football teams played their major bowl games on January 1st, and I spent that New Year's Day at Janet's home. She arranged with her family that at half-time of one of the games, everybody would leave the TV room except her dad and me; that was my cue.

Suddenly, I found myself alone with Janet's dad and knew it was time. Although her dad was bigger than me, I wasn't intimidated, but my nerves were still doing cartwheels. Trying to appear cool, contrary to my true disposition, I asked him if he would allow me to marry his daughter, Janet. When he said "yes," I was ecstatic.

We planned our wedding for 4:30 PM on Saturday, June 1, 1968, since my cousin, Linda, was getting married that same day in Pittsburgh at 1:00 PM and I didn't want our mutual relatives from Connecticut to make two separate trips. I was concerned needlessly, since nobody from Connecticut made the trip to Pittsburgh except my parents.

Planning our wedding was hectic with so many decisions and Janet had the added pressure of completing all academic requirements during her final semester. I knew this was a big step for Janet and several weeks before the wedding, as a joke, I mailed her one of our wedding announcements with a hand written message saying, "Please come…" Little did I know that Janet's feet were getting cold and that she had considered canceling the wedding. Her roommate even told her that she didn't think she should be getting married; fortunately for me, she ignored that advice.

Long before pre-nups were popular, Janet wanted me to promise her that if our marriage didn't work out that we would divorce. Knowing she needed assurance, I agreed, but in my heart I believed we'd remain together.

We had a wedding party of seventeen, including my roommate, Gary, and Janet's roommate, and aside from locking my keys in my car at the church, the wedding was flawless. We were simply too young to appreciate the gravity of those familiar words: "...for better or worse, in sickness and in health, for richer or poorer, till death do you part." With the passage of time, however, every word has become a grim reality.

We postponed our honeymoon a couple days to attend Janet's graduation from Carnegie-Mellon two days later, June 3rd. She graduated with her Bachelor of Science degree in Fashion Design and Retail. We honeymooned at Nag's Head, North Carolina, for about a week, but cut it short by a day and returned to our first apartment in Pittsburgh as husband and wife.

8
THE EARLY DAYS

THE FIRST SUNDAY after our honeymoon, I dressed to go to church and Janet was baffled; she asked me what I was doing. I told her that as a Lutheran I was accustomed to going to church on Sundays and wanted to go, but quickly assured her that she didn't have to go with me. Her parents attended church sporadically, although they took their children to Sunday school. However, if the four siblings were quiet enough on Sunday mornings, they often avoided church altogether. Nevertheless, Janet decided to join me that morning, and we went to St. Andrews Lutheran Church down the street from the graduate dorm at CMU.

During our courtship, we never talked about church or religion, but that Sunday we made an excellent decision to get involved with church and have benefited ever since.

Because I still had two more years before graduating with my architectural degree, Janet took a job working at the prestigious Horne's Department store in downtown Pittsburgh as an assistant buyer. About three weeks later, I met Janet after work for dinner and we were waiting in a line outside a steak-house type restaurant.

The person behind us in line, Duane McDonough, struck up a conversation. He asked if we were going to the crusade that evening. What crusade? Apparently, Billy Graham was at the Pitt Stadium. We were unaware of it, but at Duane McDonough's urging, we went.

Billy Graham was captivating; he gave a stirring evangelistic message and when the singers started with "Come As I Am," Janet immediately left her seat and went forward. Being a Lutheran I thought I knew everything and remained. However, things were set in motion.

The next day Duane went to Horne's Department looking for Janet and found her.

As they talked, it soon became apparent that Janet was despondent about her job, and he asked if she had prayed about it. Janet told him that she had never prayed in her life and didn't even know how to pray. Duane told her that God is like a person and she could speak to Him as she would with anybody. Was it really that simple?

When he left, Janet immediately sought out the one place of privacy available—the ladies' room. She went into a stall and said her first-ever prayer, "God, if you're really there..." She went on to say how miserable she was about her job, but that she had to work to support us since I was still in school, and she didn't know what to do.

After her first-ever prayer, she opened the door to leave the ladies' room, and her boss happened to be walking down the hall directly toward her. When he saw Janet, he asked if they could talk. Janet looked at him as though seeing a ghost; she had just prayed and now her boss was right there and wanted to talk. That was not by accident.

He made the observation that she seemed to be unhappy and suggested that it may be better for her to work the floor selling for a time and not be in the position as assistant buyer. Clearly, Janet realized that would be a demotion and finally asked if she could simply quit her job and leave. "Yes."

Immediately, Janet stood up, said goodbye, and walked out of Horne's Department Store. She then telephoned me to say that she had just quit her job. Excitedly, she told me how she prayed for the first time and knew her quitting was a God thing. What could I say? Furthermore, Janet felt that if God waited any longer to answer her first-ever prayer, she may not have connected meeting her boss with that prayer. As it was, she knew that God arranged that encounter and was now free, although unemployed.

Janet attended Carnegie-Mellon as a Fashion Design and Retail major on the urging of her dad who reasoned that because she was good with sewing and knitting, she would be great in fashion design. That didn't happen. Janet always loved children and even had pictures of them plastered on her dorm room walls. She immediately contacted the placement office at CMU looking for other employment and said that she wanted something that involved helping people.

The only job available was teaching mentally handicapped children on closed circuit TV at Western State School and Hospital in Canonsburg, Pennsylvania—Perry Como's hometown. As daunting as this position appeared, Janet still needed to work and applied for the job. It helped that Janet was attractive and her boss was a guy. She was hired. Together, they developed a program called "Janie's Farm" and Janet taught those mentally challenged children on closed-circuit TV. Thus began Janet's teaching career.

It must be mentioned that her paternal grandfather was a high school principal, her uncle a mathematics professor at MIT, her aunt was a career teacher, and Janet's dad was an attorney. Somehow, teaching was part of her genetic code; she's a natural-born teacher, as time would reveal.

I completed my coursework and graduated from CMU in the spring of 1970 with my architecture degree. On the bulletin board was a job offer from an architectural firm in Palm Beach, Florida. Surprisingly, I was the only graduate architect to apply. Why anyone would prefer living up north when there was an opportunity to relocate to sunny, South Florida? However, since Janet had just enrolled at Duquesne University in Pittsburgh to get her Master's Degree in Special Education, I wrote to the Palm Beach firm requesting that it hold my application for two years until she graduated.

My first job as a graduate architect was with Carl G. Baker, Inc., the architectural division of Michael Baker, Jr., Inc. in Beaver County, Pennsylvania, at that time the third largest architectural/engineering firm in the country.

Meanwhile, Janet fulfilled her heart's desire and became pregnant with our first child. Julie was born on September 7, 1970—Labor Day that year—in a Pittsburgh hospital, and looked surprisingly like me. She was delivered with forceps, and her head was traumatized. I witnessed the entire birthing from behind a picture window with a nurse standing nearby holding a bottle of smelling salts in case I fainted, however, I remained upright. Julie was a delight and extraordinarily bright.

The early 1970s were a turbulent time with the Vietnam War, drug use, and the genesis of the woman's liberation movement, and we were profoundly affected. Janet not only became a student once again, but also a woman's libber. There was a time when she took a bus trip from Pittsburgh to New York City to march with the woman's liberation protestors down Fifth Avenue.

Our marriage became strained. By this time, we had moved to Sewickley, west of Pittsburgh on the Ohio River, so I could be closer to my job. Unfortunately, there were no churches to our liking in the area so Janet held awareness-raising meetings in our rental home for the feminists in the area. Janet's sister, Claudia, attended.

It was ironic that when Janet hosted a feminist meeting, Claudia's husband, Mark, and I would visit the local bars to enjoy looking at the female dancers gyrating to the song "Sweet City Woman," among others, and certainly never thought of "liberating" any of them. Janet's choice reading material at the time was *Ms.* magazine while mine was *Playboy*. We were not on the same page, and things were going downhill. Sadly, Claudia divorced Mark at that time, but when Janet considered leaving me she asked herself what kind of man she wanted. She listed all the qualities that appealed to her and came up with...yours truly. We remained together.

9
FLORIDA BOUND

Much to my surprise, after nearly two years the Palm Beach archi-tectural firm wrote back and asked if I was still interested in relo-cating to Florida. How often does that happen? One of the principals of the firm graduated from Carnegie Tech years earlier, and he was my point of contact. In late spring of 1972, I took a flight to Palm Beach, met with Gene Lawrence, the founder of the firm, and he offered me a position as a project architect. Construction was booming in Florida.

Meanwhile, Janet had just graduated from Duquesne with a Master's Degree in Special Education and was offered the job of her choice in Pittsburgh. Yet, she, too, took a flight to Palm Beach to scope out her job market, but nothing was available.

On her return flight to Pittsburgh, when the pilot announced that they were passing over the Ohio River and Janet saw nothing but air pollution, she knew it was time to relocate. Those palm trees, blue skies with end-less sunshine and the beautiful Atlantic Ocean looked mighty attractive by comparison. Within days I gave my notice at Carl G. Baker and Associates, and three weeks later we arrived in West Palm Beach. It was Saturday, August 5, 1972, sunny and blazing hot.

This was a bold move since Janet had the job offer of her choice in Pittsburgh and there was nothing was available in Florida. On the last day of summer vacation, however, the Palm Beach County School Board tele-phoned Janet and offered her a position teaching mentally handicapped children, ranging in age from four to fourteen. This position was available because it was in a low-income area and nobody wanted it. Janet accepted it as we needed the money.

At that time the schools in Florida were light years behind northern counterparts.

While up north, I was the co-project architect for a 70,000 square foot special education school that had astro-turf in the four separate play-grounds. The school where Janet taught didn't even have air conditioning in her classroom and it was summer in Florida.

It took us several months, but in early 1973, we discovered Nativity Lutheran Church in Palm Beach Gardens and began attending regularly. The people there became our church family and we found ourselves doing everything with our new friends.

Not surprisingly, raising Julie was challenging at times. While she was like me physically and mentally, emotionally she was the complete opposite. She was strong-willed, while I'm the compliant type, very easy going. Obviously, our precocious two-year-old usually wanted things her way. We used a noted child psychologist's book to help raise Julie and he believed in letting the child express herself. That didn't always work.

One spring day in 1973, Janet simply needed a break and went to the swimming pool at our apartment complex while I watched Julie. When Julie awoke from her nap, she wanted Mommy. I told her that Mommy was gone for a while, but that I would be with her. Apparently, I wasn't good enough…she still wanted Mommy. I then took Julie to my car and told her we were going for an ice cream cone. Bribery usually works, but not this time. *She wanted Mommy!*

I was unaware of it, but there was volcano building within her little two-year-old mind which finally erupted with a vengeance. She lunged at me and clamped her little two-year-old hands around my neck to choke me. Where did that come from? As bad as that was, what I did was probably worse. I took her to see Mommy. Who was running our family? That noted child psychologist's advice failed us.

In the spring of 1974, Janet became pregnant with our second child, and at the same time, we bought our first home in North Palm Beach with three bedrooms, two baths and a swimming pool—vintage Florida.

Janet wanted a natural childbirth, so we took the Lamaze classes together and were ready for the main event, but sometimes life is anything, but routine. Janet went three weeks beyond her due date and was finally induced to deliver Laura on December 10th.

We have since learned that when a baby arrives late, the head begins to harden and is not that pliable coming down the birth canal. Janet experienced the greatest pain in her life while birthing Laura and I witnessed every painful moment of it. Fortunately, Janet rebounded quickly, soon forgot the pain and focused on our new baby girl. She was fair, like Janet, very outgoing and perfect in every way.

Janet took a maternity leave to deliver Laura, but that was the year of the world-wide oil embargo with its crushing effect on business. The

Lawrence Group employed 26 people in 1974. By 1975 it was down to eight and I was *numero ocho* (number eight). Gene Lawrence even told me he would have to let me go, but for whatever reason, he never did.

With such a tenuous hold on my job, however, we experienced the pressure of job insecurity which compelled Janet to return to teaching in early 1975. Ever so reluctantly, she had to leave our beautiful infant daughter, Laura, in the care of a church friend, Ronda Danielson. Janet could not be that stay-at-home mom she had always dreamed about and was truly broken-hearted. The only good news was that Ronda turned out to be an exceptionable surrogate mother.

10
CURSILLO

IN JANUARY OF 1976, my friend Kirt, Ronda's husband, invited me to attend a rather strange sounding weekend in Miami called "Cursillo." Cursillo (Cur-SEE-yo, accent on the second syllable) is a Spanish word that means "short course," and this was a short course in Christianity. I was not a hard sell for Kurt and he seemed surprised that I agreed so quickly. Another church friend, Jim Groth, told me to have fun. Somehow having fun at a Christian weekend seemed incongruous.

At the beginning of that weekend, the rector (leader) said that each of us would get out of Cursillo what we put into it. Isn't that true about everything in life? Since I wanted to maximize my experience, I threw myself into all activities.

As a Lutheran, I attended church weekly and knew all the stories about Jesus Christ, only it was all head knowledge. Most people considered me to be a good person by their standards, their human standards; yet, God the Father would judge me by a different standard, His holy standard.

I have since learned that because of the Fall of Man, I was doomed, born with a sin nature. Thank you, Adam. At least that explains how my precious daughter, Julie, would know to put her little two-year-old hands around my neck to choke me. Nobody taught her because it was natural as she, too, was born with a sin nature.

But God the Father did something that is simply hard to believe. Knowing I was helpless with my sin nature to ever have a relationship with Him, He sent to earth His own son, Jesus Christ, born as a human being who lived a life without sin, and willingly shed His blood as a sacrifice to atone for the penalty of my sin and the sin of all those who would believe in Him (John 3:16). When Father God now looks on me, He sees me sinless, washed clean (metaphorically speaking) by the blood of Jesus and I am now able to have a relationship with Him, calling Him Abba, meaning "Daddy."

At that Cursillo I finally realized what Jesus had done for me and received Him *in my heart* as Lord of my life; I became *born again* (John 3:3). *My life has never been the same.*

And did I ever have fun. After every meal there was a joke session with the only requirements that the joke be short, clean and funny. Everybody roared!

When Kirt took me home that Sunday evening after Cursillo, I was emotional when I told Janet that I had just met Jesus and received Him in my heart.

Janet, meanwhile, was struggling. She was taking three college courses at night to get certified in elementary education to teach 'normal' children, still taught full-time, was a mother to our two young daughters, a wife to me, and was hanging on by finger tips.

However, in May of 1976, she, too, attended a Cursillo in Miami and the Lord touched her heart. On Monday, the next day, Janet went to work and her friends noticed a perceptible change; she seemed to be glowing. They asked her what happened and she told them of her born again weekend with Jesus. *Those Cursillo weekends changed both of us.*

After our experiences Janet and I immersed ourselves in Cursillo activities with church friends. Although we attended our weekends in Miami, there was a new organization, the Goldcoast Cursillo Center, just starting in Boca Raton, Florida, about 35 miles from home. Both of us met weekly with our respective small groups, women for Janet and men for me. We attended monthly gatherings with people from the entire Goldcoast community, volunteered to help with activities during week-ends and were blessed to be selected for Cursillo "teams." Together, Janet and I have been on about twenty "teams" and each of us has been the rector (rectora for Janet) for a Cursillo weekend. God showered us with His grace.

One of the activities during Cursillo is for ordinary people, lay people as opposed to clergy, to give a variety of talks during the weekend. I was always uncomfortable and even fearful about speaking in public, although several people tried to help me.

While a senior in high school, my history teacher asked me to give a talk for the American Legion. She even arranged to have the speech teacher tutor me. While it helped, I was still a bundle of nerves when I delivered the talk. When the teacher telephoned my home to ask if I would do it again for another group, my mother said "no!" She knew public speaking was not my forte.

Gene Lawrence even paid for a fellow architect and me to take the

Dale Carnegie course in an effort to get us more comfortable with public speaking. I can't say that worked, either.

Yet, when asked to give a talk on a Cursillo weekend, everything changed. Why? While praying about it, I believed the Lord wanted me to deliver His message and if He wanted it, then, somehow, He would help me through it. Simply put, I trusted God!

That first talk lasted about thirty minutes, but it seemed as though I was suspended somewhere in God's twilight zone as time stood still—what a trip! The Cursillo even had a name for that experience: "actual grace." That's when the Holy Spirit flows through somebody enabling that person to do something beyond his natural abilities.

With the Lord's help, I overcame my fear of speaking in public.

One Cursillo weekend that stands out was, ironically, in Pittsburgh. Janet's brother, Richard, who Janet sponsored to Cursillo years earlier, was the rector and asked me to give one of the talks. After praying about it and sensing an affirmation, I agreed. It was a forty-minute talk and I diligently prepared and prayed fervently for grace repeatedly. Part of the preparation included writing the entire script. When I delivered that talk, however, I fixed my eyes on the people listening and barely looked at the script. I had never done that before.

At the team meeting later that evening, one of the team members was incredulous at what he just saw and asked me if I had memorized my entire talk. I simply told him, "No…I lived it!" I have since learned that to teach anything, preparation and praying fervently are a dynamic and powerful combination.

One of our most unique Cursillo experiences was at the Union Correctional Institute, the maximum security prison, in Raiford, Florida. This is where death row inmates are executed. As we were about to meet the prisoners for the first time, their chaplain reminded us, "They're not here for singing too loudly in the church choir!"

Janet and I, along with our Cursillo friends from church, attended about four or five monthly meetings at Raiford in 1978. The trip to Raiford took about six hours and we left at 4:00 AM to be there on time. Hearing the steel doors clang shut behind us was always a sobering experience, but once we were with the Christian prisoners, it was church. While it was grueling physically, nobody ever complained; we were blessed to hear testimonies how the Lord was active even behind prison bars. The majority of those prisoners were not much different from any of us. I've heard it said more than once, "There, but for the grace of God, go I."

In December 1978, I had the privilege to be on the team for Cursillo #4 at Raiford. Seated at my table group was the notorious jewel thief "Murph the Surf." Jack Murphy and his partner stole the Star of India sapphire, the largest in the world, from the Museum of Natural History in New York City in 1964, in true James Bond-style. However, he was incarcerated for murdering a woman in Miami.

Jack Murphy intrigued me. He gained his reputation as a jewel theif, but was also a champion surfer and, of all things, a concert violinist. However, God Himself touched Jack Murphy's heart and changed him. He was miraculously released from prison several years later and began his own prison ministry.

Seeing how the Lord could change a person's life was the motivation for not only me, but for all of us involved. Janet and I were active for nearly seven years and the only reason we ended our Cursillo activities was that God moved us to a different church with no Cursillo connection. Life does move on.

11
JOB WOES

WHILE I WAS soaring spiritually in the late 1970s, vocationally I was troubled. Early in 1978, I became increasingly disgruntled with my job at The Lawrence Group. I felt unappreciated and certainly miffed that my salary did not keep pace with my responsibilities—sounds like a familiar tale of woe. What made it worse is that I was not communicating with Gene Lawrence which only exacerbated the situation.

With so much negativity in my mind, I began looking for another job. There was another firm in the area that was highly respected and did some noteworthy architecture. In fact, several people in the past had left The Lawrence Group to work for this firm. Finally, I contacted one of the principals and, over a period of time, he agreed to hire me at the salary I sought. Although I was still not communicating with Gene, I had to tell him I was leaving for another job. That conversation did not go well. We always had a close relationship and it was now ending.

On my last Friday at The Lawrence Group, I still had not communicated my grievances with Gene—talk about an elephant in the room—but something odd happened. That afternoon Janet had a doctor's appointment in West Palm Beach on Flagler Drive by the Good Samaritan Hospital. When her appointment was over, it was late afternoon, but traffic was so heavy, she could not make a left turn heading home. Spontaneously, she turned right and drove to my office in Palm Beach, only minutes away.

As Janet entered the reception area who should happen to see her, but Gene Lawrence. Gene was always fond of Janet, so he immediately took her into his office and asked her one question, "What happened?" He was genuinely baffled. Immediately, Janet knew she stepped into the middle of something beyond her comfort level as she felt Gene's pain. She left his office, found me and said, "You must talk with Gene."

I saw the writing on the wall and, ever so reluctantly, went into Gene's office. After months of silence, I finally had a good heart-to-heart talk with him. It cleared the air (at least for me), but created another problem. Though we had reconciled, I couldn't back out of my commitment to begin working with the other firm on Monday. As difficult as it was, I boxed-up up my supplies, said my farewells and left The Lawrence Group that Friday afternoon with a heavy heart.

Monday, I went to my new job. It was a beautiful office, very professional, and I even had my own cubicle. There were about ten or eleven architects all working in the same area, each with his own cubicle, and I was the low man on the totem pole, since I was the last one hired. There was one secretary to do all the correspondence for the eleven or so architects, my peers, and all letters had to be reviewed by the principals. One of the principals gave me my first project, to prepare the preliminary drawings for a detached bank drive-through in Palm Beach.

By Wednesday, I couldn't stand it any more. What had I done? Surreptitiously, I telephoned Gene and arranged to have lunch with him the next day since I wanted my old job back. I knew that this was a major decision in my life and didn't want to blow it, so I prayed. Immediately, I sensed a tremendous peace. I stood up, turned completely around observing everything in that office, and realized one simple truth. I did not belong there.

Over lunch the next day with Gene, he agreed to my salary request and welcomed me back. We were both pleased. Furthermore, the project he assigned to me was the Esplanade Worth Avenue, a 90,000 square-foot retail center on the 100 block of Worth Avenue anchored with a Saks Fifth Avenue store at one end, valet parking at the other end, underground parking (which was always a problem with the high water table) and even rooftop parking. Of course, I had my same office, and Gene trusted me to write my own letters without proofing them.

All of this was made possible because the Lord used Janet's spontaneity to bring about reconciliation between Gene and me at the eleventh hour on that Friday afternoon. Although I was gone for two weeks, when I returned, I didn't miss a beat and began my duties as project architect for the Esplanade Worth Avenue. It was a challenge and I thrived.

The following spring, 1979, was the beginning of the headaches, and I became that walking time-bomb. The Lord carried me through that perilous time and I survived brain surgery quite well by the grace of God. By mid-August, I was well enough to resume my full-time responsibilities as project architect at The Lawrence Group.

12
HURRICANE

I T WAS LATE summer of 1979, less than three months after brain sur-gery and Hurricane David was bearing down. That hardly seemed fair. Having never experienced those ferocious winds before, Janet did her best to control her anxiety and I tried my best to calm Janet.

Hurricane-force winds and rain were destructive enough, but there were other perils. Wind driven objects—coconuts, tree branches, pebbles from gravel roofs or any loose items—suddenly became missiles speeding horizontally at nearly 100 miles per hour. Our windows were particularly vulnerable.

Some of the windows had storm awnings which were easy to protect, but the remaining windows were unprotected. Our Florida room overlooking the swimming pool had nearly thirty feet of jalousie windows which were not even watertight, especially with horizontal rain under great pressure from hurricane-force winds.

Fortunately, I felt well after brain surgery and knew it was my responsi-bility to protect our home. The easiest way to shield those vulnerable win-dows would be to purchase sheets of plywood, cut them to fit over those windows, and fasten them in place. At least it sounded easy. The plywood was not heavy, but after hours of lifting and fastening the panels in place, my shoulders were sore. No surprise there since I used muscle unaccus-tomed to lifting for hours.

Hurricane David struck on Labor Day and was a Category 1 with maximum sustained winds of 95 mph. Our landscaping suffered minor damage, but our home remained safe.

We all went outside as the eye passed overhead. It was like a block party with neighbors milling around just to experience the stillness of the eye, but it didn't last too long as the winds started picking up again for Act II of David and everybody scuttled back to the safety of their homes. After the storm, I removed the plywood panels.

Weeks later I began to experience pain in my shoulders. What caused this pain? I dismissed any thought that installing those panels caused the pain since David blew by weeks earlier, and the human body is an amazing machine that heals itself quite well. The only thing I was doing differently was taking Phenobarbital, that anti-seizure drug. Attributing a drug for causing shoulder pain may sound far-fetched, but nobody really knows the side effects of any drug until time passes.

With the passage of time my shoulders deteriorated. By December I could barely lift my arms above my head as there was significant joint pain; it was difficult to even shampoo my hair.

Janet has an unusual skeletal condition called Arachnodactyly (spider fingers, in layman terms) and saw a very bright rheumatologist, Dr. John Whelton. He helped her with joint problems. Now, I had my own severe joint problems in both shoulders and made an appointment to see Dr. Whelton in January 1980.

When he examined me, he diagnosed me as having bilateral adhesive capsulitis—"frozen shoulders." It sounded dreadful, but he did something that truly astonished me. He injected both of my shoulders with Cortisone and overnight my pain disappeared. I never expected such instant relief and have experienced no shoulder pain since that day. Thank you, Dr. Whelton.

13
THE SPIRIT'S SURPRISE

EARLY IN 1980, Gene Lawrence summoned me into his office and said that since I was the project architect for the Esplanade Worth Avenue (which had been completed months earlier), he wanted me to investigate cracking on the rear wall near the valet parking. Dutifully, I walked across the street to the Esplanade, went downstairs to the basement garage and inspected the rear wall. There were no cracks. Then, I went outside to inspect the rear wall at grade level, but again, saw no cracks. Obviously, Gene was bright and wouldn't send me on a wild-goose chase, but I wondered what he expected me to analyze since I didn't see any cracks. I was clueless and dejectedly walked back to the office to give Gene my observations, or, more accurately, my lack thereof.

Once I entered his office and sat down at his desk, Gene became temporarily distracted, so I closed my eyes and silently offered this simple prayer, "Lord, what caused the cracks?" I was unprepared for what happened next.

Immediately, in my mind's eye, I saw a picture of what caused the cracking.

This had never happened to me before. The Holy Spirit just gave me my first *word of knowledge* (1 Corinthians 12:8) and I was stunned. (This word of knowledge was literally a supernatural revelation by the Holy Spirit who graciously answered my desperate prayer to discover what had caused the cracking; in my mind's eye He showed me the scene of how it happened even though I wasn't there.)

When Gene looked up, I nonchalantly told him what the Holy Spirit had just shown me. "The contractor was loading concrete block on the second floor at that location of the building. The problem was that the concrete hadn't cured to its maximum strength; it was 'green concrete' and the weight of the block overloaded and weakened the concrete beams at that location causing the cracking."

Gene immediately perked up and said, "John, you're absolutely right because the cracks are occurring from the top down and not from the bottom up." I'll admit it, I felt like a hero, but the Holy Spirit got the credit since I was the clueless one and He showed me exactly what happened. I couldn't tell Gene how I knew this, since he likely would not understand, nor did he ask me; however, that revelation was precious.

At Easter time that year, Janet and I made the bold move to change churches, and this was difficult for me. We had been at Nativity Lutheran Church for seven years, but our pastor had been promoted to bishop for our district and had been replaced by a much younger and inexperienced pastor. Also, Janet began meeting people from Cursillo with a variety of backgrounds and was hearing about a Spirit-led life. This piqued Janet's curiosity.

For several months Janet attended a local charismatic Roman Catholic service on Wednesday nights to get more of God. I never went because I often had a headache. The leader of this group went to Maranatha, a local Church of God, and being ever inquisitive, Janet finally persuaded me to visit Maranatha on Sunday mornings—after attending Nativity Lutheran.

It was certainly different, but, over time, I began to enjoy the upbeat music and the pastor was a superb Bible teacher. Janet and I began soaking up the Bible like sponges; however, leaving Nativity Lutheran was difficult because our friends were there and by leaving, we would be severing our relationships. Nevertheless, a woman we recently befriended at Maranatha encouraged us to join with her and we did.

Often, it's not easy to follow God, but we knew we made the right decision. Janet and I each bought our own Ryrie Study Bible and, over the years, wore them out by studying. The Bible became our handbook for living and guide for raising children. That noted child psychologist was out and the Bible was in.

Although Maranatha was a radical change for me, another appeal was that the church often had outstanding guest speakers, one of whom was Ben Kinchlow, the co-host on Pat Robertson's *The 700 Club*. He gave his testimony describing how he became a Christian, which Janet and I never forgot. He was a seeker looking for a way to live and prepared his own spiritual litmus test with three questions: Was it real? Did it work? Did it work *now*? Christianity answered those three questions affirmatively and he embraced it all.

14
ANOTHER BABY AND PARENTING

In the spring of 1980, Janet had that gleam in her eye; she wanted another baby. I wasn't thrilled about her idea as I was content with two beautiful daughters and suggested we pray about it. Secretly, I felt that with the Phenobarbital flowing through me, the chances of Janet getting pregnant would be slim. (Janet's older brother had difficulty impregnating his wife while on Phenobarbital after his brain surgery.) Nevertheless, we prayed about it. I was being magnanimous and gave Janet, and perhaps the Lord Himself, one month to get her pregnant. Have I mentioned lately that life is full of surprises?

I believe the first time Janet and I were intimate after praying, she conceived. When we realized what had just happened, my entire attitude flipped when I recognized the Lord was at work once again. This would be our only child conceived in prayer.

Because of the difficulties from the two previous deliveries, Janet and her doctor agreed to have a Caesarian section. She was given the choice of having our baby either the day before or the day after Christmas. Janet chose to spend that Christmas at home.

Peter was born the morning of December 26, 1980. Unlike his two older sisters, Peter missed the trauma of birth, and I missed seeing Peter being born, since the C-section was surgery and I was not allowed to be there. I had witnessed both Julie's and Laura's births. Only minutes after Peter was born, however, our pediatrician, holding our newborn in the crook of his arm like a football, brought him to me and showed me our son. The C-section was the easiest of her three deliveries. He was fair like Janet, active, and so good-looking. One person commented he had the best features of both of us. Peter was named in honor of the passenger we met in the limousine on June 12, 1979, and during my Cursillo, I sat at the table of Peter. He completed our family.

To be good parents requires love, patience, and, of course, sacrifice. In the spring of 1982, Julie put me to the test. She and I were together in our back yard, and, for whatever reason, she was angry. While standing on our old brick barbeque, she yelled: "You and mommy don't love me!" I was speechless and my first impulse was to rebut her angry outburst. Since I was the adult and much bigger than my eleven-year-old daughter, I could have screamed back even louder and said, "Of course we do!" But I remained silent. Intuitively, I sensed that Julie needed an attitude adjustment and not merely mental assent; attitude changes take time.

In response I did two things.

At that time Julie wanted to earn money by delivering newspapers for *The Palm Beach Post*, our local newspaper. While that sounded tempting (my brother George and I were both paperboys), what kind of parent would allow an eleven year-old, a girl at that, to deliver newspapers early in the morning? She never considered the dangers of riding her bike, usually before sunrise. There was a little boy in Florida named Adam Walsh who was abducted and murdered less than one year earlier. There were unseen dangers out there when it was dark, especially of the two-legged variety, and I simply wouldn't let her do it alone. Instead, I offered to deliver papers with her.

Her route consisted of 90 customers, one block to the north, south, east, and west of our home. We were virtually at the center of her route and every morning the newspapers were dropped off in our driveway. So, my ambitious eleven year-old got her wish. She earned her money, but together we bagged the newspapers, loaded my car and delivered them as I drove. On some days I let her sleep in and delivered the papers myself; she appreciated that. Julie has never again questioned whether or not her mom and I love her. We showed her by our sacrifices. We delivered newspapers together for the next five years.

My second action was to pray, "Father, how could I love Julie more?" Immediately, the Holy Spirit actually spoke to me. It wasn't in an audible voice, but I *heard* these words distinctly in my mind, *"Fast desserts."* What? How could my fasting desserts help me to love Julie more. My mother was not only an outstanding cook, but an outstanding baker as well. She made desserts from the "old country"—Slovakia in Central Europe—that people only read about, like the strudel with paper-thin dough that's stretched over a large, flat table before putting in the various fillings. I admit it, I have a sweet tooth. Nevertheless, I attempted to fast desserts.

Janet and I have attended a number of conferences by Bill Gothard, an outstanding Christian counselor from Chicago, and one of his statements is forever ingrained in my memory, "What the parents do in moderation, the children do in excess." If I have any habits, good or bad, guess who watches, learns and imitates? The children, of course! Eating desserts is not bad, unless God tells a person specifically to fast desserts. Julie picked up my desire for desserts and, for being a picky eater, she surely enjoys her cookies and ice cream. Although I tried to fast desserts, I ultimately failed. We have both suffered from that failure.

Years later, those words of Bill Gothard began to haunt Janet and me in a different area. She and I enjoyed a glass of wine before dinner several times a week. With those words of "moderation" and "excess" echoing in our brains, we did not want our moderate indulgence to influence Julie and Laura, our teenaged daughters, to drink excessively. We were not concerned about Peter because he was still young. As a result, we decided to abstain from drinking and, for the next seven years, touched not a drop of alcohol. We believe our abstinence established a healthy role model for Julie and Laura, since they have never abused alcohol.

Later in the summer of 1982, we were planning to visit my parents to celebrate my mom's birthday. I prayed about what present I could give my mom and, once again, the Holy Spirit immediately answered me with one word, *"Shave!"*

After Cursillo I had grown a beard, perhaps to identify more with Jesus, but it was wiry and not at all attractive. My mom never cared for it, but would never interfere in my life by telling me to shave. When the Spirit told me, however, I obeyed and shaved. When Mom saw me that summer, her entire countenance lit up and she smiled in sheer delight. That was the best present I could have given my mom.

15
LAID-OFF!

Losing a job is like an accidental death—unexpected, sudden, and final. I had been with Gene Lawrence for more than a decade when he called me into his office and said, "I have to let you go." Those words rocked me. Gene was more than a boss, he was my benefactor—the one who offered me a job in South Florida, as well as a friend. Business was slow in January 1983—although it was worse in 1975, when Gene kept me—but there were other dynamics at work.

A month earlier, Janet and I met with our pastor because we were both dissatisfied with our jobs and contemplated leaving. He gave us this rather profound, but practical, counsel: "You both can't quit!" We didn't, although I was laid off soon after talking about leaving. Apparently, it was my time to move on.

After leaving the office for the last time that afternoon, I rallied my emotions and actually became giddy with anticipation; I expected something good to happen. Understandably, Janet was shocked when I told her and envious that my job was over and hers wasn't, although getting new employment was a definite priority.

Early the next week, I telephoned Gene and asked him to put in a good word for me with the Canadian developer who had just completed Crystal Tree—a 120,000 square foot retail/office complex in North Palm Beach. I was the project architect for Crystal Tree and knew the project intimately and worked closely with the developer's team. I would be perfect to become the interface between the developer and new tenants although he had just hired a person for that position.

Gene graciously contacted the developer for me and within a week, I hit the jackpot. The developer did hire me to become the interface which was synonymous with being a problem solver. Our home was only three miles away, part of the jackpot.

My position didn't stop with problem solving since new tenants needed architectural drawings for their tenant improvements. That wily developer knew he just hired an in-house architect as well as a problem solver.

However, I came face-to-face with an unexpected dilemma.

While working with Gene Lawrence for over ten years, I did no architectural design. Gene was the designer, and I was a project architect. My responsibility was to take his design and prepare the architectural drawings for bidding, obtaining a building permit, and constructing the project. I worked extensively with Gene—the designer—consulting engineers, building officials, and sometimes with owners, and coordinated all architectural drafting, but did zero design.

At Crystal Tree, when a tenant would approach me to discuss specific program needs and style, I'd better produce a design that met the requirements with a touch of dazzle, or else I wouldn't last long. It was like standing on a precipice knowing one bad move could send me over the edge, hardly a comforting thought.

Very much aware of my shortcomings, I prayed fervently for creativity. From a Christian worldview I believe that God created the world and everything in it and that He is enormously creative—think hammerhead shark. The Bible states that I'm created in His image (Gen. 1:26–27) which encouraged me to express my dormant creativity.

My first tenant design was for a woman from Montreal who wanted a lingerie boutique. Ask me how many of those I've designed and you already know the answer…a big, fat zero. Nevertheless, through much prayer, my design was a stunning success. She even asked me to design a boutique for her in Montreal, but that never worked out. Nevertheless, I hit the ground running with newfound confidence. With God I *can* do all things. (Philippians 4:13)

After my day job with the developer I did architectural drawings for tenants in the evenings. I set up my drafting table in the small office I shared with Kathleen, part of the management team at Crystal Tree. Although the office was crowded, we made it work.

Coincidentally, ten years later my family and I moved to a different community where, unbeknownst to me, Kathleen and her family had been living. We've been neighbors for the past twenty years; it is a small world.

As an architect who's experienced so many lean times, I simply couldn't refuse people who solicited my services. Consequently, I accepted projects unrelated to Crystal Tree which made no sense whatsoever. I was already overloaded with work and making more money than ever, yet I took on more. Greed did not motivate me, perhaps it was fear, but I felt I was a superman who could take on the world. I arranged with a local architect in West Palm Beach to use his office for my personal projects which needed to be separated from those at Crystal Tree, usually from midnight on. There were too many sleepless nights.

People were not designed for non-stop work; I needed sleep and simply wasn't getting enough. Also, I discovered a subtle facet about adrenalin. A person can push his body to stay awake by using stimulants, medications, or even sheer willpower, but adrenalin is not a switch that can be turned off at will. Too many times in the wee hours of the morning I crawled into bed physically exhausted, but was unable to sleep because my mind was still racing. Eventually, when I did conk out and woke up hours later, my heart was often pounding and my eyes showed the fatigue. The warning signs were evident.

Finally, in September 1983, I saw Dr. Neil Ozer, an internist, who has since become my primary care physician, and he gave me my first-ever stress test. After chugging up that incline with all those wires monitoring my heart, he made the observation that I was on a path of self-destruction. Simply put—sleep was good, sleep deprivation was bad. I made the most money ever that year, but at the expense of a potential physical breakdown. Nevertheless, I heeded his advice, reduced my workload and slept at night.

16
HOMECOMING

IN MID-OCTOBER OF 1983, Janet and I planned to travel to Pittsburgh to attend her fifteen-year college homecoming. She was usually homesick at that time of year to enjoy the brightly colored leaves and cooler temperatures, and often manipulated her schedule so she could travel north. At the same time we arranged to swap vehicles with her dad, who often went to auto auctions to pick up a bargain. At our request he purchased a pre-owned work van that we planned to customize for our family.

Our children were thirteen, eight, and two at the time, and earlier that spring Janet and I went on our first ever Western Caribbean cruise during her spring break. Having people watch our children that week went as smooth as silk, and we had a fabulous time cruising. What happened that October, however, was the antithesis. Julie and Laura whined about our trip and didn't want us to leave. We had to do our own family damage control to pacify them even though we had arranged for Julie and Laura to stay with their best friends and Peter with his sitter.

Since it is a more than 1200-mile road trip from North Palm to Pittsburgh, Janet and I set out early Thursday morning traveling north on I-95. Being the good wife, Janet offered to drive, and I let her since Florida is flat, relatively straight, and likely the easiest to drive. However, as she began driving, she perceived something was wrong with the car. She felt a vibration or movement in the front end and sensed yellow flags waving vigorously. I never noticed anything, but I'm a guy. She reduced speed, drove on the shoulder of the road, and exited as soon as possible. Quickly, we found a service station with a mechanic and pulled in.

By now, we were accustomed to life's little surprises and that day gave us a whopper. After explaining to the mechanic what we perceived was happening, the mechanic put our car on his hydraulic lift and raised it. As he raised the car, the right front wheel wobbled. *Wheels rotate, they aren't supposed to wobble.* The mechanic told us later that something had sheared off on the wheel and it was virtually hanging on by a thread. Fortunately, after about two hours the mechanic made the necessary repair and we resumed our road trip.

Janet and I realized that with the difficulties we were encountering, we both considered whether or not there were demonic forces trying to hinder or even prevent our trip; it surely seemed that way. Consequently, as Christians, we were even more eager to press forward to our anticipated spiritual conflict and continued northward.

After spending the first night in a motel on the road, we finally arrived at Janet's home in Wilkinsburg, a suburb of Pittsburgh, about 5:00 PM on Friday, October 15th. Janet's mom and dad greeted us warmly. I paid my father-in-law the money for the van and after refreshing about an hour, we drove to the home of one of Janet's brothers for dinner.

It was a family reunion—Rich and Wendy and their four children, Willard (Janet's other brother) and Susan with their son, Janet's mom and dad and, of course, Janet and I. Any time Janet's family gets together for a meal, it's usually loud and raucous, and this time was no exception. Later in the evening, Janet's dad returned home alone while Janet's mom remained with us at Richard's to spend the night.

The following morning was an idyllic October day—sunny, crisp, invigorating, simply good to be alive. Nana (Janet's mom) telephoned home early that morning, but there was no answer which was not unusual since Papa (Janet's dad) often went out for breakfast. About mid-morning Nana, Janet, and I drove back to Wilkinsburg to begin our day. We parked across the street from her home, and Janet exuberantly picked up some fallen autumn leaves and tossed them in the air. She could hardly contain her joy. However, I felt uneasy; something was wrong. The newspaper was still in the front yard and the screen door was locked. Undaunted, Janet declared, "I have perfect peace."

We opened the front door and the house was eerily silent. While her mom and I remained downstairs, Janet enthusiastically bounded upstairs looking for Papa. She looked in the master bedroom and was surprised her dad made the bed which is something he never did, but he wasn't there. Janet then went down the hall glancing in the other bedrooms, but he wasn't in those either. As she was about to walk downstairs, Janet noticed the hall bath door slightly ajar and casually opened it. *That's when she screamed!* She just found Papa—naked, hunched over the toilet—*dead*!

He had suffered a massive heart attack the night before and died instantly. He was a big man (6'3" and about 260 pounds) and was certainly not in great physical shape, but the evening before he seemed perfectly healthy and fully enjoyed the family activities.

Janet came downstairs terribly shaken, and I ran upstairs to assess the situation. Sure enough, he had been dead for probably ten to twelve hours and his body actually had a mottled look to it, like autumn leaves when they change colors.

This was an incredible shock for Janet's family. Nana, however, was saved from the worst grief because she had remained with us at Richard's house the night before, though she and Papa were rarely apart at night. If she was there when he keeled over and died, we don't know how Nana would have handled that alone. We suspected it would not have gone well. As it was, when she learned of Papa's death, Janet and I were with her and immediately comforted her.

I thought it interesting that only Janet and I viewed her deceased dad; no other family members, who had joined us by this time, had any desire to go upstairs and see Papa with that mottled look. When Janet telephoned her sister in California and told her that their dad had just died and that she found him, Claudia asked the obvious question, "What are you doing there?" Obviously, God had a different purpose for Janet and me to make that road trip and it certainly wasn't to enjoy a college homecoming or swap vehicles. We experienced a homecoming, but it was Papa's and not at Carnegie-Mellon University.

Papa was 70 years old and seemingly in decent health, yet he died within hours of our arrival in Wilkinsburg. Was our being there merely a coincidence? I doubt it. The Bible indicates that our days are numbered (Psalm 139:16) and that the Lord directs our steps (Proverbs 16:9). Our trip was really intended to protect and comfort Nana, which we did and the rest of the family as well.

An interesting side note is that Julie telephoned Papa about 10 PM the evening of the 15th because she had a burden to talk with him. She was likely the last person to speak with him alive.

The wake and the funeral were surprisingly upbeat because everybody recognized that our being there was part of God's plan. Also, only three weeks earlier, Richard witnessed to his dad about accepting Jesus as Lord of his life and he did.

The funeral would have been a fitting conclusion to our homecoming chapter, but there was more to come.

On our return trip we drove south through West Virginia and passed over the New River Gorge Bridge. When that bridge opened in 1977, it was the longest steel arch bridge (3,030 feet long) and the highest vehicular bridge (876 feet high) in the world.

As I began driving across the bridge, that's when it hit me...*paralyzing fear*. Thoughts began bombarding my mind of turning the steering wheel ever so slightly and crashing over the side plunging to certain death. I've heard of soldiers on a battlefield becoming paralyzed with fear and at that moment my mind became a battlefield for our very survival. Janet was beside me in the passenger seat and Julie and Laura (who had taken a flight for Papa's funeral) were sprawled out in the back of our van. I did not want to wipe out my family with any sudden jerks of the steering wheel, but everything was happening too fast and I was near panic. I was driving over 70 miles per hour with no place to stop. What would I do?

Desperate to survive, I locked my eyes on the road directly in front of me and repeatedly said the name "Jesus" in my mind. We shot across that bridge safely, but that's an experience I never want to repeat. By the grace of God, it's never happened again.

Years later I related this incident to my pastor at the time and he thought a spirit of death from Janet's dad may have attacked my mind while crossing that bridge. Janet thinks that I suffer from a fear of heights. I'm more inclined to believe the pastor as I did experience a spiritual attack which may have been what Janet and I considered at the beginning of our road trip.

One interesting fact in this episode is that the civil engineer who designed the New River Gorge Bridge was the Michael Baker Company, the company I left eleven years earlier to work in Palm Beach, once again proving that it's a small world after all.

17
CHANGES

Early in 1984, the developer of Crystal Tree urged me to lease space in their office tower and open my own architectural practice. Did I have a choice? I suppose I could have declined, but the developer offered to pay for my first office build-out and since I had zero assets, I accepted his offer. Although I would no longer be the interface working for the developer, he would continue to pay me for any tenant improvement drawings at Crystal Tree. We were both satisfied.

Opening up my own architectural practice required many decisions. I joined the American Institute of Architects (A.I.A.) thinking it would help to promote business and, most importantly, incorporated as John M. Nossal, A.I.A., P.A.

One tiny decision was the design of my title block which identifies the name of the architect, his address, telephone number and a logo of his choosing. I had been using a logo of a stylized fish (which early Christians who were persecuted secretly used to identify themselves to other believers). Since I was about to purchase 200 pre-printed mylar drafting sheets, I was undecided whether or not to continue using the same logo. Being undecided, I simply asked the Lord in prayer whether or not I should keep the fish.

Was I being too trite or irreverent? The Bible says the God even knows the number of hairs on our head (Luke 12:7). If He's so interested in us to know the number of hairs on our head, I figured that my prayer about my title block wasn't *that* trivial.

He answered me the next morning. While shaving, I happened to look down in the sink and one of my hairs—number unknown—had fallen from my head and landed forming a perfect stylized fish. I stared incredulously; what a unique way to answer a prayer. With total confidence I ordered the pre-printed sheets with that stylized fish as my logo. Having the Lord's blessing, I've kept that logo ever since.

Opening my brand-new office was exhilarating. It wasn't big; there were two offices each with windows—one for me and one for drafting, a small conference room, a storage room with a print machine and a reception area. I was able to furnish it inexpensively and displayed my business card at a local Christian book store owned by friends from Cursillo. Tom, a draftsman and fellow believer, phoned me looking for work and I hired him. We worked together nearly seven years.

In January 1985, I developed a health problem; it became painful to urinate and there was blood in my urine. I promptly made an appointment with a noted urologist and he diagnosed me with prostitis, an infection of the prostate. He prescribed for me an antibiotic and within days I began to feel better.

Unfortunately, after weeks of being well, I began to suffer with the same symptoms and visited the urologist again. What was causing this infection? He had no good answer, nor did I. Nevertheless, with additional antibiotics I was cured a second time and became healthy once again.

Several months later, I attended a Maranatha Men's Retreat. After breakfast on Saturday morning I ate two of the most delicious, giant-sized glazed doughnuts imaginable. After lunch, I did likewise and was biting into my second glazed doughnut when the Holy Spirit once again spoke to me clearly in my mind, *"That's your problem."* Immediately, I knew what that meant. *Excessive sugar was causing my prostate problems.*

My urologist didn't know, I didn't know, but the Spirit knew and just told me. I experimented the following weeks and, sure enough, if I ingested sugar, my prostate began to act up. When the Lord spoke to me in 1982, about loving Julie more by "fasting desserts," I never realized how that would benefit me. Now I knew. I reduced my consumption of desserts, but still never fasted completely.

18
EMOTIONAL TURMOIL

E ARLY IN 1986, Janet began to have an emotional meltdown. She would be 40 that spring, but peace eluded her. Fortunately, there was an inner-healing ministry at Maranatha led by Richard Daniels, a friend of ours. Richard was a painter by trade—he painted our home years earlier, but was also gifted in praying for people with emotional turmoil.

On Thursday evening, February 6, 1986, we arranged to meet a friend of ours at one of Richard's meetings. At the last minute, however, Janet and I decided not to go and telephoned our friend, but she wasn't there. To keep our word, we felt obliged to go.

That evening changed our lives, not because of anything Richard said or did, but that was the evening we met Larry and Elaine Lambert.

Larry was in his late fifties, very handsome with white hair and reminded Janet of her dad. He accepted Jesus as his Lord and Savior at the age of 47 and absolutely threw himself into Christianity. He routinely attended four or five church services on Sundays in Orlando and became passionate about the things of God.

Larry and Elaine began attending Maranatha only months earlier, but already acquired a reputation for helping people with emotional problems. At that meeting we sat directly in front of them and Janet was nearly jumping out of her skin. Afterwards, she introduced herself to Larry and Elaine and burst into tears. None of us knew why. Larry was very calm and kindly suggested that Janet meet them privately and thus began a journey none of us could ever have imagined.

About the same time, Janet made an appointment with a renowned counselor in Boca Raton we knew from Cursillo. After his initial session with Janet, he diagnosed her as a victim of sexual abuse. How could he diagnose her so quickly? Everything Janet said and did fit the profile of a woman who had been sexually abused.

It didn't take long for the Lamberts to unravel the mystery in Janet's life. Beginning at the age of three, Janet had been sexually abused. How could a three-year old possibly cope with abuse with no defense mechanisms?

Close your eyes…block it out…it doesn't exist. Janet had total amnesia; she remembered none of the details. Yet, memories that evade the conscious mind get buried in the sub-conscious, which never forgets.

Identifying an emotional problem is a vital first step; healing it becomes the challenge.

We knew a woman from Maranatha who had some psychological problems and was under the care of a psychiatrist for three years to attain a measure of healing. I thought to myself that, surely, it wouldn't take Janet three years to be healed; I was so naive. Janet received ministry from Larry and Elaine for nearly three years, but that was merely the first stage of healing; more was coming.

That time was the most tumultuous of our marriage. I never knew who would greet me after work; would it be Janet, my loving wife, or some stranger in a distant place hiding in her own cave? All those emotions that had been buried for decades were now being exposed, causing a clinical depression in Janet that was incomprehensible. Clinical depression is so much more than a bad-hair day.

One day, Janet was baking a turkey when she laid the scalding oven rack on the floor of our kitchen and inadvertently leaned her foot against that rack. While her flesh sizzled, *she never moved her foot!* She got a third-degree burn—the most severe kind—but Janet's depression numbed her brain's response to pain. How could that be? *She was a walking dead person.*

Janet saw a doctor who treated her for the burn and he pleaded with her to return for a follow-up visit…for free. Her wound could easily have become infected and he was desperate to heal her, but walking dead people really don't care.

On another occasion, a Saturday afternoon in October 1986, I was working in my office at Crystal Tree when Janet phoned to say she was flying out to San Francisco to stay with her sister, Claudia. She couldn't stand the emotional upheaval churning inside her and wanted to escape. In psychological terms this was a "fight or flight" conflict and Janet was literally planning to fly.

While talking with Janet on the phone, I experienced severe pain in my left arm and told Janet I was having the symptoms of an impeding heart attack. Because of those symptoms, Janet never left. I believe the Lord knew that would be one way to keep Janet grounded and not flee. I've never had any problems in my left arm or heart since that occasion.

Many months later, once again, Janet was planning to fly to San Francisco to be with Claudia. Intuitively, I knew that if she left, I would likely never see her alive again. She was so unstable. How could she possibly care for herself when living was so hellish? Since she wasn't listening to me, I rounded up Julie, Laura, and Peter and sat them down in our sitting room for an impromptu family gathering. If Janet was so determined to leave, then she would be the one to tell our children.

It was a tearful meeting, but once again, Janet remained home. Even in her depression, her love for her children overrode the agony of her depression.

There were other times when her self-esteem was so low that she felt unworthy to even sleep in our bed. On those occasions she slept on the floor at the foot of our bed curled in the fetal position. Nothing I said or did offered her any cheer. She suffered in a dark place alone.

Christianity is a great comfort in times of distress, but seemingly nothing worked. None of the promises in the Bible seemed to fit Janet's situation and we were both at wit's end. However, Janet and I clung to hope—hope in God when there is nothing else to embrace (Psalm 42:5). By the slimmest of threads, hope carried us through this bleak valley with, seemingly, no end in sight.

Janet has a remarkable story of survival, but that's hers to tell and not mine. Suffice to say that we've still married, love each other as well as the Lord; He never did stop loving us.

19
BUZ

WHILE THIS WAS the beginning of the darkest period of our marriage, Janet still taught as teaching took her mind off her emotional turmoil (at least temporarily), I continued my architectural practice at Crystal Tree and our three children attended school. We did our best to live normally. However, by this time, Janet was burned out with teaching, and, in May 1986, offered her own prayer: "Lord, if you want me to leave teaching, you'll have to do a miracle in John's business."

Two or three days later, the Lord provided that miracle. While sitting in my office I took a telephone call from Buz DiVosta, the largest developer in our area, and he asked me if I wanted to do some work for him. What? How did he even know me? *We had never met!*

"Yes!" I almost shouted.

Everybody in Palm Beach County knew of Buz DiVosta. He was a giant among developers. Every year his company, Burg & DiVosta, was one of the Top 100 Builders in the nation as determined by *Builder* magazine, the professional periodical for the industry. His homes were in such demand that people camped out to be first in line simply to buy one. Conversely, I was a relatively unknown architect quietly doing tenant improvements at Crystal Tree or elsewhere in South Florida.

Burg & DiVosta had just completed the Bluffs Square Shoppes, a strip shopping center in Jupiter, Florida, serving one of their communities with over 2600 dwelling units. There was already a Publix supermarket, a Walgreens pharmacy, a bank, and a Toojay's—a New York-type delicatessen—but there were still vacant tenant spaces that needed architectural drawings.

My first project and "test" was a Hallmark card store. Apparently I passed, since Burg & DiVosta commissioned me to prepare the architectural drawings for the remaining thirteen tenant spaces, including a 200-seat restaurant, named McCarthy's. Tom, my draftsman, and I were giddy with work. I even hired another draftsman to meet deadlines. Since the

Lord delivered the miracle that Janet requested, she took a year's leave of absence from teaching.

I've speculated that one of my clients from Crystal Tree, who interviewed with Buz DiVosta for space at Bluff's Square Shoppes, may have shown him architectural drawings we had prepared and he liked the drawings; that may have been the point of contact.

Tom and I completed our work for the Bluff's Square tenants in the fall of 1986, and he casually asked what we would be working on next. I was unsure myself, but simply said, "The Lord will provide." And provide He did. In October one of the vice-presidents at Burg & DiVosta offered me the position as Chief Architect with Tom as Chief Draftsman. As tempting as it was to accept on the spot, I restrained myself and replied that as a Christian, I needed to pray about it.

I did pray for guidance and sought counsel from many people. Not everybody was in favor of my accepting this position and each one had valid reasons. Also, one of my other clients was Southland Corporation, which owned the 7-11 stores. I had done renovations on about a half dozen 7-11s from Miami to Vero Beach and my relationship with Southland looked promising for the future.

When I asked Janet, my most trusted spiritual adviser, to pray about this decision, she reminded me of a dream she had. She had dreamt of a cookie cutter making batches of cookies. Those cookies were identical, made repetitiously and done quickly. That precisely described the Burg & DiVosta construction technique.

Being incredibly innovative, Buz DiVosta purchased quick-release steel forms from a company in France for pouring concrete walls and decks. They were perfect for the four-plex units he made popular in South Florida. A day after pouring the fast-setting concrete, the forms were released, cleaned. and set on another slab and the process was repeated; it was done speedily.

The detached single family homes were similar; the design was identical with minor variations to the garage roof trusses, color, 'opposite-handed,' and having either a front- or side-loaded garage. Those homes were desirable because of their value and solid construction.

The image of the cookie cutter could not have been more appropriate. Ironically, my daughters, Julie and Laura, and my brother George lived in a Burg & DiVosta four-plex at different times.

After a month of seeking counsel and prayer, I had peace and notified

Burg & DiVosta that I accepted their offer and began the process of shutting down my practice at Crystal Tree. Everything went smoothly. My first day as Chief Architect was the Monday after Thanksgiving, 1986.

About two months later I took a phone call from Dean, my contact at Southland Corporation and he told me a rather sad tale. Southland Corporation had a major corporate shake-up and stopped all capital improvements, meaning construction activity, for the foreseeable future. Dean then asked me for a job, but I could not help him.

Yet, I almost never made it to Burg & DiVosta.

Anybody in South Florida who does yard work is familiar with fire ants. These little buggers are only an eighth of an inch long, but pack a wallop! I've been bitten often, and it feels like fiery needles pricking the flesh—and who likes that? Then the blister forms and is filled with pus. It is one horrible insect bite.

Sometime in October, 1986, I was standing in my driveway wearing sandals when, suddenly, I felt the "fiery needles" in one of my feet. Immediately, I reached down and squished those four tiny fire ants that seemingly bit in unison. How do they do that? I was annoyed, but never gave it a second thought. Since I had an errand to run, I drove away.

While returning home about forty five minutes later, I began to feel funny and looked in my rearview mirror only to get the surprise of my life. Who was staring back at me? My entire head, including eyelids, nose, lips and ears, were grotesquely swollen! I looked like an alien, something one would see on the cover of a sensational tabloid. Those four tiny fire ants apparently injected their venom into a vein in my foot and I was experiencing anaphylactic shock!

What to do? Where to go? I should have driven directly to the emergency room at the Gardens Hospital, which wasn't too far away, to get a shot of Benedryl or Epinephrine. Instead, I drove home and telephoned Larry Lambert, whom I had gotten to know quite well by this time. Although he lived in Jupiter, about thirty minutes away, he promptly drove to our home in North Palm Beach and, upon arriving, prayed vigorously for my healing.

Janet, meanwhile, had arrived home and saw me at my worst...the alien look. While my head and features made me unrecognizable, *by the grace of God* my trachea never swelled to the point of cutting off my air supply. Otherwise, I wouldn't be writing this account. The swelling finally dissipated and I survived yet another close encounter with the Grim Reaper. *Thus concluded my harrowing experience number three!*

20
LARRY AND ELAINE

SOMETIMES BEING TOO successful creates a problem for others. Larry and Elaine hosted a "home group" that had grown to nearly 100 people. While Janet saw the Lamberts every week for counseling, we hosted our own home group and never went to theirs. When one of my friends told me the Lambert's group was like a church, I thought that he surely must have been mistaken, until I saw for myself.

There was praise and worship music, a teaching, and an offering. It *was* church. Because of the numbers, this home group met in the clubhouse of a local condominium. Clearly, there was jealously from some other home group leaders, as well as awkwardness with the pastoral staff. A church within a church was a threat. As a result, in the spring of 1987, the senior pastor at Maranatha shut down the Lamberts' home group and their ministering to any people from church.

The Lamberts had no other job or income other than ministering to people in need. One of those people happened to be Janet. At precisely this same time, a former pastor and his family relocated from Michigan to South Florida and were introduced to the Lamberts through mutual friends. Because Larry and Elaine were shut down, they bonded with the former pastor and agreed to start a new church approximately twenty miles north of Maranatha. What would Janet and I do?

In any counseling situation, to separate the counselor from the counselee is simply ill-advised. We had no choice; we were attached at the hip to Larry and Elaine and couldn't leave them. It was painful to leave Maranatha since I was a deacon and the architect for the recently completed Maranatha Christian Academy, an 8,550 square foot private Christian school adjacent to the church. Our daughters were involved in their youth programs and I worked with the pastor to develop plans for future expansion on church property. Nevertheless, after seven years we left Maranatha to support the Lamberts. Janet even named the Lambert's new church, Church of the Living Waters.

Later that spring, Janet formally retired from Palm Beach County Schools to be that stay-at-home mom she always desired to be. Unfortunately, she was still going through intensive ministry from the Lamberts and had little peace.

Larry, Elaine, and the other pastor lasted nine months together before splitting up. Nobody was surprised since having co-pastors is often a recipe for failure. Still, those nine months were vital for Larry and Elaine's learning curve because the other pastor took them through the steps to start a church.

Immediately, the Lamberts began a church of their own with a boost from Richard Daniels and his wife Peggy, who happened to be an assistant principal at an elementary school in Palm Beach Gardens. We met at Peggy's school for services on Sunday mornings and Wednesday evenings. The Lamberts named the church "Fountain of Life" and began services in January 1988, for about 80 people. Larry was president and I was vice president.

Larry was passionate about the things of God and was a gifted motivator. In May 1988, he arranged for a group from the church to drive to the Florida Panhandle, about an eight-hour drive, to attend a prophetic conference in San Destin, Florida, organized by Christian International. One of the features of this conference was that everybody in attendance would get a "personal prophecy." What was that?

Bill Hamon, the founder of Christian International (CI), wanted to raise up a company of modern-day prophets in North America who would hear from God and minister to people prophetically. Janet and I were curious about having a "personal prophecy," but even before deciding to attend, she asked this question, "Why don't we go to the conference and hear if God would say anything about the land we're about to buy?"

Earlier that spring, we put down a deposit to purchase a two-and-a-half acre parcel of land in Jupiter Farms to build our family home. (It had always been my dream to design and build our family home.) Friends from church knew of this particular lot for sale, which, coincidentally, was diagonally across the street from another dear church friend.

About 25 of us from Fountain of Life, including Janet, Laura and me, drove to the resort in San Destin, for the conference. After outstanding music, Bill Hamon, a dynamo of a person himself, described his vision for Christian International, but the highlight for so many of us was that each person or family attending would get a personal prophetic word from a team of modern-day prophets. Each prophecy was tape recorded and given to the person. It was a class act.

Shortly into the prophecy for Janet, Laura and me, Leon Walters declared, "I see a piece of land…you will build a house…you will use the men of the church to help you build it…and you (John) are a builder."

When Janet heard those words, "I see a piece of land," she gasped! How could he possibly know that was the very reason for our being there? Modern-day prophets have an expression called "reading your mail," telling you something about yourself that only you and God know. When that happened to us, it certainly got our attention. Leon missed it when he identified me as a builder since I was an architect, though…or did he?

The land we considered buying had an inherent problem, however. In reviewing the documents for the sale of the land, my attorney discovered a glitch in the original plat; there was an error of 50 feet. In no uncertain terms, he told me I wouldn't know the exact boundaries of this property and would likely have difficulty securing a mortgage. However, I was undeterred.

If God, through the prophet, said I was going to build a house, would something as insignificant as a 50-foot error on two and a half acres ever slow me down? Never! Frustrated with my resolve, my attorney, another friend from Maranatha, finally wrote a one sentence letter in half inch high script, "DO NOT BUY THE JUPITER FARMS PROPERTY." Admittedly, it was impossible to miss his intent, so I did the next best thing, I ignored it. I have been called immovable, and this time it was a whopper.

The Bible says that man plans his way, but the Lord directs his steps (Proverbs 16:9). What that meant is that my plans may not always prevail.

On a Friday afternoon that June, I took a telephone call from the owner of the property, who said he needed a decision that day on whether or not I would buy his property as he had another buyer. No problemo. Immediately, I telephoned the banker with whom I had been talking and his secretary told me rather matter-of-factly, that he had just left for the weekend and was not available. Immediately, I saw my dream crumble before my eyes as I could not purchase that land to build the Nossal home. I was crushed.

"So are My ways higher than your ways" (Is. 55:9) and for nearly a year from that fateful Friday afternoon, Janet and I couldn't even look at any other property. Since time heals wounds, however, eventually we felt well enough to search once again.

We phoned a realtor friend and he showed us some lots in what he described as a "sleeper community," meaning it was a little out of the way and few people had even heard about it. That was our introduction to River Ridge in Tequesta, Florida.

It was a gated community having full-time security with approximately 175 home sites, each with approximately one-third acre, and it was located on the north fork of the Loxahatchee River. Jonathan Dickinson State Park was located directly to the north, which would never be developed. That same Saturday afternoon, May 15, 1989, we signed a contract to purchase Lot 41.

Bill Gothard had a similar experience. He related how his ministry near Chicago was growing and he needed land to expand. In prayer he heard God tell him to purchase some land from his neighbor, a farmer who owned much of the surrounding property. When Bill Gothard approached the farmer and asked to buy some his land, he encountered a belligerent person who told him in no uncertain terms that he would never sell him any of his land. That was a crusher and perhaps Bill Gothard questioned whether or not he heard God correctly.

Several years later, however, while totally unsolicited, the same farmer approached Bill Gothard with a different attitude and asked him if he was still interested in purchasing some of his land. He answered with an enthusiastic "yes!" They completed their land deal and years after originally hearing from God, Bill Gothard finally got the much needed land for expansion.

Bill Gothard named that type of experience as a "Death of a Vision." That is, when God tells a person to do something, he goes for it only to hit the figurative brick wall, but with the passage of time, God's word is resurrected and consummated.

This is exactly what happened with our land purchase. We believe we heard from God through the prophet, went for it, only to hit the wall, and were left dazed and confused. Yet, a year later we purchased another parcel of land, far better than the first, only it was in God's timing and direction, not ours. His ways *are* higher than our ways.

21
MOVING ON

W HILE OUR ORIGINAL land deal collapsed in the spring of 1988, our older daughter, Julie, graduated from The King's Academy (TKA), a private Christian school in West Palm Beach, and enrolled in Lee College in Cleveland, Tennessee.

Since Janet was living her dream as the stay-at-home mom, a teacher no less, she home-schooled Laura and Peter that fall semester as other families in our church did. It seemed like such a good idea, but evolved into a colossal failure. Peter (7) complained the birds made too much noise and he couldn't concentrate. Laura (13) simply didn't want to get out of bed, let alone study and Janet herself was getting 'cabin fever' after being home two-and-a-half years. They were all miserable.

By December, Janet had completed her counseling with the Lamberts after nearly three years and became fairly normal once again. Since our attempt at home-schooling was a flop, we enrolled Laura and Peter in local Christian schools. The first day after Christmas break in January 1989, Janet drove both Laura (8th grade) and Peter (2nd grade) to their respective schools. She returned home, sat down on our living room sofa and said out loud rather sarcastically, "Well, God, now what are You going to do?"

Immediately, the telephone rang and it was The King's Academy and the caller asked if Janet would come in for an interview. Janet was stunned. She had applied to substitute at TKA, but subs did not need to interview. What was happening now?

Unbeknownst to us, TKA had just fired a third grade teacher and was desperate to hire a replacement.

At that time Janet was meditating on the scripture, *"The steps of the good man are ordered by the Lord…" (Psalm 37:23).* Janet drove to TKA, was interviewed for the job and shown the classroom. On the bulletin board was that exact scripture, *"The steps of the good man are ordered by the Lord…"* A plum just dropped into Janet's lap.

Janet was hired and began teaching third grade one week later. During that week, we arranged for Laura and Peter to attend TKA since one of the perks of Janet's new position is that children of teachers attended tuition-free. This was almost too good to be true; how could this happen? God directed our steps and His timing was perfect.

Janet is a gifted teacher (just ask her students), but she is also a free spirit and was now teaching, at least for her, at a virtual boot camp...rules, rules, and more rules. Nobody ever said life would be easy, but Janet not only prevailed, but excelled. The elementary teachers at TKA had a very demanding job and many didn't last very long. One year, Janet's principal told her that she was the stability of the third grade, simply because so many other third grade teachers tried teaching there, but couldn't handle the demands of the job and sooner rather than later, quit. Janet never quit.

In the spring of 1989, Peter wanted to play soccer in the eight and nine-year-old league in North Palm Beach except the league was short of coaches. One of the league's officials, a co-worker from Burg & DiVosta, *strongly* encouraged me to become Peter's coach. I had a problem with his request—I never played the game and didn't know one soccer rule. Yet, with Peter expecting to play, how could I refuse? So I offered my colleague a deal. If he could find me another parent who actually knew the sport and would be willing to become my assistant, then I'd coach.

He found one—Danny's dad from South America. Don't all guys from South America play soccer? That's how I became Peter's soccer coach. The first season was forgettable, but the second season was promising. I was excited because there were two boys on our team with cannons for legs, probably the best in the league.

Peter played goalie and for the first three games we were undefeated. Our next game was against the other undefeated team in the league, the Sting. Regardless of the age or the sport, there's just something about competition that gets the adrenalin flowing and I was pumped. There were three periods to each of our matches and our team, the Gators, had a penalty kick. I had Danny (with a cannon for a leg) take the kick and he made it. We led 1-0 as the first period came to an end.

Here's where it became interesting...the Holy Spirit spoke to me! I heard very clearly in my mind the words, *"Change your defense."* I thought, "But Lord, a 1-0 lead will probably not hold up, we need to score more goals." I didn't change our defense. In the second period the Sting scored two goals and led 2-1. The Sting coach changed his defense beginning the third period and we lost the match 2-1, our only loss of the year.

I told that story to a pastor and his wife we had invited to dinner and the wife said incredulously, "God doesn't care who wins a soccer match between eight and nine year olds!" She was probably right. God probably didn't care who won that soccer match, but He was vitally concerned about obedience and I just failed that test. Those words—*"Change your defense"*—were more of a command than suggestion. Through sheer naiveté, I argued with God thinking I knew better and the outcome was predictable. Sometimes, I wonder if I had changed our defense whether or not we would have prevailed and enjoyed an undefeated season. Obedience to the Lord is always the right choice; I was still learning.

In the spring of 1990, Janet and I took the bold step to sell our home of 16 years. We simply wanted to be closer to Fountain of Life Church, which by this time had leased a storefront in the Jupiter Park of Commerce, and, with our children growing, we needed more space.

Accordingly, we contacted another realtor friend we knew from Maranatha who listed our North Palm Beach home. Sadly, she was unsuccessful in selling our home and when her contract expired, we didn't renew it. Somehow, Janet felt all along that we would sell our home ourselves. We planted a 'For Sale by Owner' sign in our front yard and then waited. Within weeks somebody expressed an interest, but it wasn't a buyer, but a friend of the buyer.

A youth pastor had taken a job at a church in North Palm Beach and searched the area for a suitable home for his wife and three young boys. He was unsuccessful and returned to West Virginia empty-handed, but had others in the church continue his search. One of the other pastors' wives noticed our sign, liked the neighborhood and stopped by for a tour. She thought our home would be perfect for their new youth pastor and even made a video to send him. She was our point of contact.

While Janet was praying one day about the sale of our home, she heard the Lord tell her not to 'quibble' about the price. That was an interesting choice of words. How many people use the word "quibble?" In a long distance telephone conversation with the youth pastor, however, he told us he didn't want to 'quibble' about the price! That sealed the deal. We sold our home to that youth pastor, sight unseen, on August 27, 1990.

22
THE AX

T HE AX FELL January 4, 1991. That was the day I was laid off from DiVosta and Company in the midst of another recession. Unlike eight years earlier, I experienced no good vibes for future work, although I was the primary support for a family of five, with Julie a junior in college. While the economy was listless, the bills were endless. Janet remained a third-grade teacher at The King's Academy, only their pay scale couldn't match that of public schools. Financially, we took a severe body blow.

Buz DiVosta had always treated me well and, even for this layoff, waited until after the Christmas break to release me. My severance package included several month's salary, and when I asked for my drafting station—drafting table with light and stool—he gave those to me. I've always had a great respect for him; he is visionary—keenly aware of the big picture as well as knowing the nitty-gritty of construction details.

After the sale of our North Palm Beach home, we rented a house at the Hamptons at Maplewood, a DiVosta community in Jupiter. I was the architect for our rental home as well as 6,500 other dwellings—either single family or four-plex units—and Phase II of Bluff's Square Shoppes, including a 150-seat restaurant originally named Black Diamond Grill.

By this time Janet and I had gone to a couple conferences by Christian International (CI) and always found the prophetic words to be accurate and edifying. The very next week after my layoff, there was another CI conference. With nothing crowding my calendar, I made the long drive to the Florida Panhandle to hear what God, through the prophets, might say about my job loss. I was the only person from our family or church attending this conference, but received a personal prophecy that was eerily poignant.

There were four people who prophesied over me and I was comforted knowing the Lord had a purpose for this job loss. Two of them actually told me the same thing, "John, you've fought your lion and the bear and now you're facing Goliath. What will you do with Goliath?" Most people know the story of David slaying the giant Goliath. However, before David slew Goliath, he had previously slain the lion and the bear. That gave him a measure of confidence to stand up to the giant Goliath and ultimately slay him. How did the imagery of the lion and the bear and even Goliath possibly relate to me?

On June 15, 1979, I had brain surgery at the Presbyterian Hospital, Columbia's medical school. The school mascot for Columbia is the lion. While David slew the lion, I went through my brain tumor experience expecting God to deliver me from death, which He did. Together, we slew our lion!

The perpetrator of Janet's sexual abuse had a picture of a grizzly bear hanging on the wall of his bedroom. It took nearly three years, but we slogged through that first stage of healing with the Lamberts ministering to Janet. Together with the Lamberts and our hope in God, we slew the bear!

Facing unemployment with a family of five…was this my Goliath?

Another person who prophesied said that I was up to elbows in alligators, hardly a comforting image. He continued by saying I was very educated, analytical and knew what I was doing, but everything was on a downward spiral with nothing working. Then he told me the reason why I was laid off; that was rare. He said God was molding me into *a man of faith*, but with a smirk, quickly added that in prophetic terminology, the way a man of faith is developed is that he'll *walk on the brink of disaster*. Oh no! In other words I'll need to trust God even more in my life.

When I had the brain tumor in 1979, the Lord Himself encouraged me to trust Him as He led me through the entire sequence step by step. Consider the following:

- I never expected that my last headache would be on Friday, May 25, 1979, three weeks before surgery, but God did.

- I never planned to see Benny Hinn three times in a span of five days, the last time within 24 hours before learning I had a brain tumor; but God arranged it.

- I never anticipated an affirmation from a retired neurosurgeon that my doctor would be one of the best, all because of a stranger named Peter, who I *happened to meet* in a limousine, but God orchestrated that ride.

- I never selected my actual neurosurgeon, Dr. McFarland, since I had interviews with two neurosurgeons on June 12, 1979, but God chose.

- There was no way to determine whether my tumor would be benign and not require chemotherapy or radiation either pre-or post-surgery, but God knew.

- I could never predict that the day after surgery, while recovering in the Neurology ICU, that nurses would wheel in a television set for me since I was so cognizant and alert, but God healed me.

- I never expected that less than three months after brain surgery, I would be well enough to board up my windows to protect us from Hurricane David, but God strengthened me.

And I was the walking time-bomb!

It was through events in my life that the hand of God was so evident that they elevated my faith. But *He* primed my faith pump. *He* took the initiative. *He* built my faith in Him, step by step.

Janet's experience with the healing of sexual abuse was much different than my brain tumor, but with the same result. It built our faith. Dark valleys are somber places; nobody ever wants to remain there. We were in that valley nearly three years and what sustained us was our hope in God. *"Yea, though I walk through the valley of the shadow of death, I will fear no evil, for Thou art with me"* (Ps. 23:4). Larry Lambert often said that we're only walking through the valley, not camping there. When it was finally over, our faith in a good God *was* increased.

Here's the kicker. Although I was laid off, I still knew that God wanted me to build our home. Who would do such a crazy, idiotic thing like building a home in a gated community with 24/7 security without a job or cash flow? That's sheer insanity. But did I believe God or not? When Leon Walters prophesied in 1988, that I would build a house using the men of the church, were they merely empty words or an event about to happen? All of us have choices. *I chose to believe that God wanted me to build our home while unemployed…that was my Goliath!*

23
CLIMBING THE MOUNTAIN

ALTHOUGH I WAS facing an impossible task—to build a house with no job or enough income to even support my family, would I quit at the starting line or go for it? I had an experience as a freshman at Columbia that inspired me.

One Friday afternoon in October 1962, I had a freshman football game at Baker Field on the northern tip of Manhattan. After the game, I planned to return home in Connecticut to see my high school girlfriend. I had checked the train schedule and found the best one, an express leaving Grand Central Station at 6:02 PM arriving in Bridgeport a little more than an hour later. Express trains were so much quicker than the local ones which stopped at every town, village, hamlet, or whistle stop along the way.

Unfortunately, I erred about the start of the game.

Our games normally began at 1:00 PM, but this one started at 1:30 PM. Thirty minutes doesn't sound like much, unless there's a train to catch. When the game was over, I dashed into the locker room and immediately looked at the clock on the wall: 4:52 PM. Decisions, decisions…what would I do? It would be virtually impossible to catch the 6:02 train since I was at the northern tip of Manhattan and Grand Central Station was midtown on the East side (42nd Street and Madison Avenue). I also had to pick up luggage at my dorm on campus and was dressed in one very sweaty football uniform. But I remember thinking, "It looks impossible, but how will I know unless I try?" I decided to go for it!

Quickly, I shed my uniform, showered, got dressed and ran out of the locker room. Time: 5:10 PM. Baker Field was at W. 218th Street/Broadway and the nearest subway stop was at W. 215th Street/Broadway. I nearly sprinted to the subway stop and no sooner stepped on the platform when the train was pulling into the station. From there I rode down to W. 116th Street/Broadway, Columbia's stop. Time: 5:26 PM. I jumped off the subway, raced to my dormitory, which backed up to Broadway, and took the elevator to the 8th floor, ran to my room, opened the door and grabbed my luggage (I did pack previously), and hustled back to the subway station toting my suitcase. Time: 5:35 PM. Again, as I stepped onto the platform another subway was just arriving. This was good. I hopped onto that subway and proceeded to the W. 96th Street/Broadway station. There, I planned to switch trains and ride the express to Times Square. As I stepped on the platform at the 96th Street station, the express was just rounding the curve and pulled into the station. I jumped onto that subway stopping only at W. 72nd Street/ Broadway before arriving at Times Square station at 42nd Street. Time: 5:50 PM.

Now there was only one more subway to catch, the shuttle from Times Square to Grand Central Station. As I ran to the shuttle platform, the subway was just sitting there, doors open, seemingly waiting for me and I leaped on. It got me to Grand Central Station within minutes, where I got off, bought my ticket and finally boarded the 6:02 express to Bridgeport. Time: 6:00 PM. I made it with two minutes to spare.

I just accomplished the impossible because every time I stepped onto a subway platform, the subway was either just arriving or was there waiting for me. If any of those four subways was more than two minutes late, there would be no story. To this day that experience has encouraged me to attempt the impossible for "with God all things are possible" (Matthew 19:26).

However, even after being laid off, the sun still rose in the east and life went on. With no work available, I did the necessary paperwork to collect unemployment benefits, and one of the requirements was that I needed to actively seek employment from three employers per week. Rejection is never easy, but I soon became accustomed to hearing those words, "Sorry, there's no work." The most awkward job inquiry was from the firm I walked away from in 1978, to return to the Lawrence Group. Needless to say, I ate humble pie in heaping portions.

Larry Lambert suggested I contact the builder which was located in the same storefront as our church. That's how I began a relationship with the local franchise of Arthur Rutenberg Homes. I introduced myself as an architect and the manager actually had a need. Whenever one of their homes was sold, the buyers typically wanted to make some minor revisions. I became the one who made those revisions on the Rutenberg drawings and became the architect of record for that particular home.

We all know how small the world is. Disney World even has the ride "It's a Small World." My predecessor as chief architect for Burg & DiVosta left to become the chief architect for none other than … Arthur Rutenberg Homes! We had even met during the spring of 1986.

Architects normally have draftsmen to prepare drawings for their projects. For the previous 20+ years, I did minimal drafting as an architect, but that was about to change. I had no employees and did all my own drafting. For the next seven years, I revised drawings for 75 Rutenberg Homes, and while this wasn't a full time job, it was a really good part-time job. Of course, for the first time ever, I set up my drafting table in our rental home and that kept me in business.

However, consider another crisis confronting me. Not only was I laid off with my income a fraction of what I had been earning, but Janet and I had bought Lot 41 at River Ridge in May 1989, sold our home in North Palm Beach in August 1990, and then I was laid off from DiVosta in January 1991. How could I possibly pay the capital gains tax from the sale of our North Palm Beach home? There was not enough money to pay bills, let alone pay the capital gains tax.

In desperation, I telephoned the offices of the Congressman from our district and the two Senators from Florida and asked one question, "Must a person who is laid off and has no income still pay capital gains tax?" In racing terms, I hit the trifecta. All three said, "Yes!"

I had a serious problem. I *was* walking on the brink of disaster.

The mother of one of Janet's third grade students at TKA was an accountant and that's how I met Karen Stedman. When I explained the predicament facing me, she did some research and discovered that if I was building a new residence of greater value than the sale of the first one, I wouldn't be required to pay capital gains tax. That gave me hope.

Yet, it takes money to build a new home. Although our financial situation was bleak, I was convinced the Lord wanted me to build our home and if He wanted it, then, somehow, He would provide the funds.

24
HOUSE OF FAITH

*N*ow FAITH IS *the substance of things hoped for, the evidence of things not seen."* (Hebrews 11:1)

Through my brain tumor experience, the Lord certainly boosted my level of faith in Him. Accordingly, as a man of faith is inclined to do, I told people that I'd be building our new home in River Ridge. I got some really odd looks, but the one that really amused me was from an engineer friend of mine. Knowing that I was recently laid off, he just looked at me with pity in his eyes. He thought I'd lost it.

Sadly, none of our church friends offered me any encouragement to build. Even Larry and Elaine felt we should continue renting. That changed dramatically, however, in January, 1992, when prophet Gary Brooks visited Fountain of Life. As he began to minister, he called out Janet and me in the presence of the entire congregation and gave us a prophetic word. He said the place where we were living was only temporary and that in a year we'd be in a much larger home and that we have a gift of hospitality. Everybody in the congregation cheered.

Janet, meanwhile, reflected on an unreal dream she had several years earlier, one she felt was from the Lord. She dreamed of people living in a large multi-level rock with water gushing through it. The water likely represented the Holy Spirit and she believed the rock represented our future home.

I had been designing and drafting the Nossal Family Dream Home sporadically during the previous year and was about seventy percent finished with the architectural drawings. Our home would be a 3,500 square foot, angular, multi-level residence with a two-story great room and three car garage.

My day of reckoning occurred Friday, February 28, 1992.

While drafting the roof truss profiles that morning, because of the various angles of the exterior walls, I was having difficulty designing those trusses when the stark realization hit me! If merely drafting our home was causing me such anguish, building it would become a nightmare. Why did

I make it so complicated? A simple design would be a whole lot easier to build and would save money, rather than having a complex design.

That afternoon I re-designed our home in a tiny thumb-nail sketch with the sole purpose of simplifying the design. How could I do it so quickly? I had been literally meditating on our family home for years and one could say I was 'pregnant' with its design.

As an art history student at Columbia, I learned how ancient Chinese artists would meditate on a scene in their mind's eye for months and literally paint the scene in fifteen minutes. That's pretty much what I did that afternoon.

As I re-designed our home in that tiny thumb-nail sketch, I was excited. Janet was not. When she returned home from TKA that afternoon and I told her about scrapping our house plans, she went ballistic.

I had just spent over a year designing and drafting our home and was 70 percent complete with the drawings. How long would it take me to complete the drafting for the new design with capital gains tax bearing down in less than six months? Once again, by faith I was walking on water!

I'm not the speediest of draftsman, but with a wife breathing fire, I became highly motivated and, once again, did the impossible. In one week I prepared the Site Plan (A-1), Floor Plans for two levels (A-2), Building and Wall Sections (A-3) and the Exterior Elevations (A-4) on drawings dated March 6, 1992, merely seven days later. Those were the drawings I submitted to the Architectural Committee at River Ridge for approval, which the committee granted.

The Nossal Family Home became a 3,000 square foot, two-story, four bedroom, three-and-a-half bath, two-car garage home with a great room including fireplace, family room, kitchen, sitting room off the master bedroom, and a two story foyer with a 50-foot-long front porch and barrel-vaulted entry. We also had a 40-foot-long swimming pool since Janet enjoyed doing laps.

Janet and I had hosted a home fellowship group weekly for the past several years which became a vital design parameter. Accordingly, I separated the great room from the rest of the home with doors to our kitchen and foyer so that our home group would not be interrupted when our children and their friends used the rest of the home. That was a perfect arrangement.

By getting the approval from River Ridge, I had just bought myself some extra time. I could now complete the drawings while seeking financing for new construction.

Janet and I realized that if God wanted to shut us down, He could do so easily by denying us financing. My best friend at the time was a bank vice president, whom I met at Maranatha, and was also laid off, ironically, exactly one year earlier than me—January 4, 1990. Nevertheless, being familiar with the banking industry, he recommended a bank noted for their good new-home construction financing programs. I took his advice and applied.

Although my employment status was pitiful…I identified myself as self-employed rather than unemployed, the application phase went surprisingly well until the end. Then reality surfaced and the bank shot us down. Frankly, I wasn't surprised.

However, my first choice for financing was a local savings & loan with which we already had a relationship—our IRA savings were stashed there. Also, my contact at the S & L was the daughter of a couple we knew from Maranatha which provided a personal connection. This S & L approved our application, and, on June 23, 1992, we closed on our construction financing. Janet and I were elated; I could finally build our new home.

Through the county building department, I pulled the building permit as an "Owner-Builder." I had never built a home before, but hired people who did. My superintendent was a carpenter from Maranatha; he had the expertise in building homes, and I became his assistant. My second carpenter and his assistant were from Fountain of Life. Another church friend did my ceramic tile and built our swimming pool. I hired several of the sub-contractors I knew from DiVosta & Company while the air conditioning sub I had known from our Cursillo days.

One profound thought struck me: *If I were still working for DiVosta, I never would have taken the time to prepare the drawings, nor construct our home.* Because I was laid off and work was sparse, I had an ample supply of that one necessary commodity—time.

Janet remained detached from the design and building stage and became my most loving critic. With the concrete ground slab poured, I was bursting with excitement to show Janet. When she saw it, however, she thought it looked too small and asked me if I made a mistake. Completely deflated, I assured her I didn't.

Then, when the shell of the home was completed—with the roof trusses installed over the wood-framed exterior walls all wrapped with plywood sheathing—the house looked huge. When Janet saw our home at that stage, she remarked that the house looked enormous and once again asked me if I made a mistake. This time I simply smiled and said, "No."

However, a real catastrophe threatened on Sunday, August 24, 1992. Hurricane Andrew was bearing down on South Florida.

I elected to build a wood frame home and on that Sunday, the building frame was complete with the roof trusses installed, but without any wall or roof sheathing. The wood frame was at its most unstable stage; any breeze would have blown it over. Was I concerned? Absolutely!

Stacked in my front yard were about fifty sheets of ½" thick plywood, but there was no time to install any of this wall sheathing. Instead I became 'Johnny-on-the-spot' with my neighbors who desperately needed plywood to protect their exposed windows. My neighbors bought every sheet of plywood that day.

Hurricane Andrew, a small, compact storm with the highest wind speed ever recorded, brutally struck Florida just south of Miami, causing enormous damage and devastation. River Ridge was spared from getting any high winds and our unstable wood frame remained intact. I'll admit it. I was relieved and construction continued.

People have observed that the anticipation of an event is often more exciting than the event itself. Janet and I experienced that excitement several weeks after Hurricane Andrew. One Saturday evening, we went to our new home and climbed onto the second floor balcony outside our master bedroom. No railings were installed and there were only a couple sheets of plywood thrown over the cantilevered framing, but Janet and I simply laid down on the plywood, looked up at the stars and marveled at what the Lord had done. The dream of our family home was becoming a reality and we wept for joy.

I'm convinced, also, that the Lord Himself had some fun with us along the way.

Unlike her mom, my daughter, Laura, has a flair for design and was actively engaged in the design process. She requested an arched window on her bedroom wall and I did it. It was a good suggestion. During construction, however, she asked if she could have a step down into her bedroom, which would have been easy to achieve as it was over the garage. I regretted not having thought of it myself, but wanted no changes during construction, likely a hold-over from my DiVosta days. Reluctantly, I told Laura, "No."

Apparently, the Lord also liked Laura's idea. Several weeks later my superintendent approached me and said rather reluctantly that there was a mistake with the wood floor trusses above the garage in Laura's room. Those trusses were six inches lower than all the other floor trusses.

That perplexed me until I looked at the architectural drawings. When I designed those floor trusses, I intended for their height to be 3'2" high, or 38", but made a mistake drafting. On the truss drawings I indicated the height of those trusses to be 32", not 3'2," a difference of 6". The Lord had just given Laura her step.

One of my faults is that I tend to be too exact and, as a builder, I have learned that being too exact may backfire. The wall cabinets over the base cabinets in our open kitchen were supported between two columns approximately eight feet apart. The bottom of those wall cabinets was high enough so that Janet and I, while standing in our kitchen, could view television in the family room. I calculated the width of those cabinets within a fraction of an inch and ordered the wall cabinets accordingly.

When the cabinets arrived, I was distraught to discover they were too wide to fit between the columns. Reluctantly, I realized I would need to cut down the sides of one or more cabinets to make them fit, but that was a 'Rube Goldberg' solution if there ever was one and these were our brand new kitchen cabinets.

However, *Somebody* once again bailed me out. The cabinet supplier made a mistake and delivered one extra cabinet. That never happens, at least not to me. There are literally hundreds of different styles and sizes of cabinets, *yet, that extra cabinet was the exact style and size I should have ordered to fit between the columns.* I have no explanation of how that extra cabinet was delivered, except to say that Jehovah Jireh—one of the names of God meaning, "The Lord Provides"—did His thing.

A minor blessing occurred when I ordered our appliance package. We didn't want the least expensive items, but certainly couldn't afford high-end appliances, either. When the time came for delivery, the vendor was out of stock of the refrigerator we ordered and substituted a significantly upgraded model. We could never have afforded that model, but received it with gratitude. Thank you, Lord.

Janet remained aloof from our home project, but the Lord gently induced her to get involved anyway. With our home nearly complete, one day as Janet was praying, she felt impressed by the Lord to walk around our property seven times praying for our home to sanctify it—to make it holy. This was similar to God instructing the Israelites to march around Jericho seven times before those walls fell down (Joshua 6:4-5, 20). She did it and walked around our property seven times praying for our home.

25
BECOMING A
GENERAL CONTRACTOR

LEON WALTERS'S PROPHECY in 1988 identified me as a builder. Although I was an Owner-Builder for our home, I would be unable to build anything else unless I had the appropriate license. Christian International taught that if there was something that could be done from a human standpoint to prepare for the fulfillment of a prophecy, do it! I certainly couldn't make any prophecy happen, but I could prepare for it when it did happen. Accordingly, I signed up to take the General Contractor's Exam given in Miami in early December 1992. By becoming a licensed GC, I would be qualified to build anything throughout the state of Florida.

However, I was so involved with building our home; I had no time to study for the exam. It was an open book test and I barely had time to even gather the twelve books necessary for the exam. I borrowed the last two books from another builder the day before the test, although both were an earlier edition than the one required.

Nevertheless, I had a plan. Instead of taking the test in early December, I would miss that one and take the next one, whenever offered. On the morning of the exam, I drove to Miami for the 7:30 AM arrival time, but was running late.

Upon reaching Miami, I encountered one massive traffic jam and for the first time rejoiced by being bogged down in traffic. I'd arrive to the test site so late, I couldn't take the exam. Yet, I also couldn't afford to sacrifice my exam fee, so I prayed, "Father, if I lose money by missing this exam, then I'll take it." There was no money to waste.

I arrived at the test site nearly one hour late, parked my car and calmly walked into the foyer where I found a test administrator. I explained to her that I was unprepared to take the exam since I arrived so late and preferred to take the next one before asking that fateful question, "Would I lose money by not taking the exam today?" "Of course!" My heart sank when I heard those two little words. The administrator quickly added, "But you're not late, they're still giving instructions."

Immediately, I turned on my heels, walked out of building to my car, gathered the box containing all twelve books and marched back into the auditorium. There were about five hundred people poised to take various exams that day and, not surprisingly, I was the last to arrive. I found an empty desk, set my books on the floor, sat down and within two minutes heard the word, "Begin."

It was a two-day exam and even though I never opened a book, with over twenty years experience as an architect and working for a successful developer, I felt confident.

One funny thing happened regarding a construction law question. I pulled out my brand new Construction Law book, opened the cover and was horrified to see the clear plastic wrap protecting the text. It would have been impossible to remove that wrap quietly. Anybody within hearing would know I never even opened the book. While it was embarrassing, I tore off that wrap and found the right answer.

Life is sprinkled with surprises and some are good. Several weeks later, I was notified that I had passed my General Contractor's Exam. It would take money to activate my GC license and since we had none to spare, it remained inactive for the next several years. God blessed me, however, by enabling me to pass that exam when I tried my best to postpone it.

I obtained the Certificate of Occupancy for our home on January 22, 1993, seven months after closing our construction loan on June 23, 1992.

Since there was still some minor work to be done, my family didn't move into our new home until Saturday, February 6, 1993. Friends from church helped us move. That date was significant because it was exactly seven years earlier that Janet and I first met Larry and Elaine Lambert. Janet believed that because of our faithfulness to the Lambert's ministry, the Lord blessed us with our new home.

From a biblical perspective, the number seven represents completeness and perfection. Our home was completed in *seven* months and we moved into it *seven* years after meeting Larry and Elaine Lambert. We never planned the time of construction or date of moving, but we know Who did! Furthermore, the Lord directed Janet to walk around our property *seven* times while praying to sanctify our new home.

It's been an incredible journey to walk by faith and design and build our family home without a job or much money. *Only* by the grace of God was I able to fulfill those prophecies that inspired me:

- by Leon Walters in May 1988...to build our home while using the men in the church—check!

- by the CI prophetic team on January 11, 1991...I was facing Goliath and what would I do with Goliath? My Goliath was building our family home by faith while unemployed—check!

- by Gary Brooks in January, 1992...the place we were living was temporary and in one year we'd be in a bigger place since Janet and I have a gift of hospitality—check!

(A famous architect once said that "God is in the details..." "David" was the first name of the two carpenters who built our home, and they helped me overcome my Goliath!)

Building our home became one of the greatest experiences of my life.

26
AWESOME GOD

L AURA GRADUATED FROM TKA in the spring of 1993, and for her class trip, toured Europe for two weeks. Money was tight, but parents sacrifice for children. Financing Julie's trip five years earlier as chief architect was so much easier. Paradoxically, Julie often reminds me that when she phoned us from Europe simply to share her excitement with Mom and Dad, I became uptight envisioning dollar bills flying away. That crushed Julie, not one of my better moments. Conversely, when Laura phoned from Europe, we chatted like neighbors. First-borns often take the brunt as trailblazers.

One of the ironies of life is that both Julie and Peter returned home from their TKA class trips on our wedding anniversary, June 1st, while Janet and I could never afford traveling to Europe.

Speaking of wedding anniversaries, our 25th anniversary that year was a dud. We had no money for anything, particularly festivities, although the church had a cake for us after a Sunday service in one of the back rooms. Not exactly how I envisioned celebrating 25 years of marital bliss, but life continues.

That November, Fountain of Life hosted an evangelist for a week's 'revival.' At that time, Janet developed a problem in her great right toe. The cartilage had worn down and she had bone rubbing against bone, which became unbearably painful. She went to a podiatrist and scheduled surgery to alleviate that pain. At the revival, however, her toe was healed, she had no pain, and, consequently, we canceled surgery. I considered that a miracle; Janet wasn't so sure.

In January 1994, my parents treated Janet and me to our first trip to Hawaii. They had been vacationing in Honolulu for the previous 16 winters and that year hosted both my brother, George, and his family, as well as Janet and me, at different times. We considered this trip a belated 25th wedding anniversary celebration.

My parents showed us their favorite sites, activities and dining venues. One of those activities was a hike around Diamond Head, nearly eight miles. My mom (80) and dad (79) treated that little jaunt like a stroll in the park while Janet and I were huffing and puffing most of the way. Hawaii was beautiful and my parents were so generous; we were grateful.

Gary Brooks once again visited Fountain of Life in May 1994, and as he had done two years earlier, gave Janet and me a personal prophecy. This one was hard to believe: "I see you (John) carrying rolls of drawings under your arm, visiting clients (which as an architect I routinely do); the name of your business is CCD—Creative Custom Design (great name for an architect-builder); I see you taking in large sums of money from your business (which I would do later), and the family is going to get $200,000.00!" Would we really get $200,000.00? It seemed impossible.

We knew it would be fruitless to guess the Lord's timetable to fulfill any prophecy. It could be weeks, months, or even years, so we settled in for the long haul.

Three weeks later, however, Janet and I celebrated our 26th wedding anniversary on Friday, June 3rd with an overnight accommodation at a local hotel on the beach. Julie's first job after graduating college in 1992 was to work as a manager at this hotel and she won the 'Employee of the Month' award, which entitled her to a free night. Instead of using it herself, she gave it to us as an anniversary present.

After taking our luggage to the room, we naturally wanted to explore our surroundings. Our room was on the third floor overlooking the pool and that seemed to be a good place to start. Since we were next to the stair tower, we walked down the stairway to the ground floor at the pool deck.

Only, we never made it.

Janet was in front of me walking down the stairway and on the last landing, only a few steps from the first floor, she fell and was in excruciating pain. She thought she broke a bone in her right foot because three years earlier she fell and snapped the fifth metatarsal on her left foot and the pain was the same.

After I sat Janet down on the stairs, I rushed to the lobby to get assistance. The hotel staff got me a wheelchair and I sped back to the stairway, delicately lifting Janet in it and wheeled her back to the lobby.

Janet needed an X-ray on her foot to determine whether or not she had broken a bone and I needed to drive her to the Emergency Room at the Palm Beach Gardens Medical Center. Since I left my car keys in the hotel room, I quickly back-tracked and went up the same stairway and noticed something that caused me to investigate. That riser (step) where Janet fell appeared different from all the others.

As an architect, I have an eye for detail and realized that if I were right, that hotel would have to pay for Janet's injury. After retrieving my car keys, I drove Janet to the Emergency Room, got the X-ray and, sure enough, Janet had a spiral fracture on the fifth metatarsal of her right foot.

Although the circumstances were entirely different, the results were eerily similar with Janet's first broken foot.

Fountain of Life was a lively church and, on a Sunday morning, there was the typical high-energy praise music with people dancing vigorously. Janet was one of those dancing. Unfortunately, she slipped and fell. Seeing her on the floor and in obvious pain, I did my best Rhett Butler imitation; I swooped down on Janet, picked her up in both arms and carried her to the church office. Within minutes our physical therapist friend joined us, examined Janet's foot, but did not think anything was broken.

Several days later, however, Janet's foot had swelled and turned various shades of black and blue. She finally visited a doctor who took an X-ray, which revealed a spiral fracture of the fifth metatarsal on her left foot.

One of the women in the church made the off-handed comment that Janet must have been in sin for such a thing to happen. We were upset with that comment, but found a measure of vindication when that same person, only weeks later, fell off a curb and broke her ankle! Be careful in judging others.

Our anniversary celebration at the hotel naturally ended abruptly with Janet's fall, but after returning from the Emergency Room, we spent the night at the hotel anyway. We talked about the possibilities of a lawsuit if that riser was, in fact, different from the others.

We checked out of the hotel the following morning, returned home and after getting Janet settled, I immediately gathered my camera, a ruler, some blank paper and returned to the scene of the accident. For the next hour or so I photographed the riser in question and, sure enough, *it was one-and-a-half inches higher than all the others.* There were two building code violations with that higher riser and we had a slam-dunk for a lawsuit.

Early the next week, Janet visited the same podiatrist who years earlier performed surgery on her left foot. The break on her right foot was nearly identical to the earlier one and the podiatrist performed the same surgery by inserting two tiny Titanium screws to connect the metatarsal.

Janet now has two screws stabilizing the fifth metatarsal bones in each of her feet.

Unfortunately, there were other complications. Because of the broken bone, Janet's foot was in a cast for weeks. For whatever reason her great right toe, the one that was healed the previous November, became chronic with pain once again. After an unsuccessful bunionectomy, Janet needed joint replacement surgery on her great right toe to alleviate the pain. The fall on that stairway landing caused Janet undeniable suffering.

By this time I had contacted my attorney about the fall and he insisted that we wait until after surgery to ascertain the extent of damage to Janet's foot. Lawsuits, even slam-dunks, take time. The hotel settled before any court appearance and I thought this would be the means to get the $200,000.00 that was prophesied, but it was not to be. However, we did receive a $100,000.00 check on August 5, 1996, exactly two years, two months and two days after Janet's fall. (I do remember dates.)

After paying our attorney, we paid off all our debt with our share of the money. This included not only our credit card debt, but also what we owed for back taxes. Being debt free was a great feeling and we even had money left over.

The following spring, I paid for our first ever Nossal Family Cruise to the Eastern Caribbean. It was early June 1997, and we sailed on the Norwegian ship "Norway" (the refurbished ocean liner originally named "SS France") and were pleasantly surprised as Caribbean cruises are so festive. Peter was sixteen at the time and delighted in mingling with all the attractive young girls who had just graduated from either high school or college. As a family, we became hooked on cruising.

27
PROPHECY FULFILLED

Fast-forward to January 27, 2000, when my Uncle Paul passed away at the age of 91. Janet and I took Mom and Dad to the funeral in New Kensington, Pennsylvania, and afterwards, met with Mick and John, my two cousins, in my uncle's home to read the will. Paul had two sisters, each with two sons and, not surprisingly, the will was remarkably symmetrical. Both sisters would get the bulk of his estate, evenly divided, while each of the four nephews would get five percent. We left satisfied knowing that Uncle Paul's estate would be evenly distributed.

My mom was named executrix of the estate, but she deferred and asked her nephew, John, to become the executor instead since she lived in Florida and he lived in Ohio, less than two hours from New Kensington.

During my childhood, my family drove to New Kensington every year to vacation with Uncle Paul and Grandpa (he passed at 92), Uncle John and Aunt Anna (Mom's younger sister) and Mick and John, their two sons. Uncle Paul took George and me to enjoy our first Pittsburgh Pirates game at Forbes Field, and it was always a delight to spend a day at Kennywood (a local amusement park).

Mick was like a second brother to me since we were the same age (he being three months older) and the same grade in school. His brother, John, was four years younger and my brother, George, was three years older. Mick and I were close.

Some surprises are brutally shocking.

Months later, John telephoned me to discuss Uncle Paul's estate. He told me that our uncle had an estate of $200,000. What!?! That can't be! My own parents had an estate of $200,000, and they had been married over 60 years, had two sons that they'd put through college, paid off their home mortgage, and traveled extensively after retirement, including vacationing 17 consecutive winters in Honolulu. Uncle Paul never married, lived in a home mortgage-free for more than 70 years, rarely traveled, spent his entire career as a manager for PPG Industries, and was frugal besides. What John told me made no sense. I said there must be some mistake.

I then phoned Mick to discuss our uncle's estate. He confirmed everything that John had just told me. I was distraught with a combination of disbelief, frustration, and anger. Unfortunately, my own brother passed away a year and a half earlier, so that meant that I would be the one to contend the will for the Nossal side of the family.

Weeks passed before I phoned John to tell him I would be traveling to Pittsburgh to personally review the banking records of our deceased uncle. He wasn't thrilled about that and thought I had no legal right to those records. There was discord between us; money was dividing even the closest of families.

Later, John phoned me to illuminate our uncle's financial affairs. He had an estate of only $200,000 because Aunt Anna convinced her brother, Paul, to put most of his money in joint accounts with her. Money in joint accounts was excluded from the estate. With those joint accounts included, however, Uncle Paul did have a sizable sum. Although he agreed to open these joint accounts with his sister, who lived merely miles away, I pondered if he realized that those accounts would be legally excluded from his estate.

Frustrated, I phoned a prominent attorney in Boston, who was part of the family, to discuss the estate and he confirmed I had no legal right to those joint accounts.

I prayed fervently for wisdom and in July 2000, wrote a four-plus page, single-spaced, impassioned letter to Mick and John telling them how I felt about the situation and encouraged them to pray about it and do the right thing. Within a week they responded. They were very gracious and said that they would give my family an additional $100,000 and a sum to George's family. While this was still less than a 50 percent division of the estate, I realized that any further bickering would be futile and, thankfully, accepted their offer.

We agreed to distribute $10,000 tax-free money as an inheritance to each of the five people in my immediate family and make the distributions in consecutive calendar years. In August 2000, Mick sent the first $10,000 checks to Julie, Laura and Peter while Janet and I waited patiently for our checks. Nothing came. Finally, I phoned him and asked about the checks for Janet and me. He said he was confused about the distribution and hadn't mailed our checks.

Now Mick is one smart person; his dad, my Uncle John, was a chemist working for PPG Industries and Mick earned a doctorate degree in electrical engineering. For him to tell me that he was confused about the distribution was hard to believe. I reminded him of our agreement, which wasn't that complicated.

What happened next was indeed tragic. Days later, Mick and his wife were playing golf and, while sitting in the golf cart, he had a sudden heart attack and died on the spot. My Uncle John, his dad, also died suddenly when his heart simply gave out at the age of sixty; Mick was only fifty-six. All of us grieved his passing.

After the funeral, Mick's widow sent Janet and me our $10,000 checks. Early in 2001, John sent us the final checks for our family's total of $100,000.

Nearly seven years after the prophecy of May 1994, we received the final amount of that $200,000 for the family. Instead of being surprised by a check in the mail, the money came through Janet's broken foot and my Uncle Paul's passing, certainly not the way I expected it.

That cliché about time healing wounds certainly happened in our family. With time, our relationship with my cousin, John, and Mick's widow has been restored to that of a close and loving family. Thank You, Lord.

28
LIFE MOVES ON

How many parents engage in that American rite of passage, driving their child to check out a college? In the spring of 1993, as I worked, Janet drove Laura to Southeastern College, a small Christian college in Lakeland, Florida, for a "College Days" experience. As routine as it sounds, it became a moment to remember. They went to the wrong college!

When they arrived, Laura was star-struck with the campus—it was magnificent. She was born with a keen eye for design, be it fashion, interior or architectural, and was delighted with the quality of its architectural design. Then reality hit. Only too soon, they discovered it was not Southeastern, but Florida Southern designed by Frank Lloyd Wright, the iconic American architect.

When they realized their mistake, they went over the tracks and found Southeastern, which was the counterpoint of Florida Southern. Southeastern's campus was formerly a retirement community and was rather bland in design (although it has since improved). While initially disappointed, once Laura met other college students there, she knew that's where God wanted her to go.

I've always encouraged our children to get involved with life and Laura took the plunge. In her freshman year she played intercollegiate volleyball and sang in the choral group. Little did I know how expensive that choral group would become.

In the spring of 1994, Southeastern's choral group was selected to represent Florida in the 50th anniversary celebration of the D-Day Landing of June 6, 1944, and the liberation of Europe from Nazi Germany. While this was a tremendous honor for Southeastern, once again, Janet and I faced the formidable task of financing Laura's second trip to Europe within a year. Yet, this was a once-in-a-lifetime experience and, somehow, we did it.

Clearly, this celebration resonated graciously with the French people who were lavish with their praise. Laura soaked it in and found herself becoming a Francophile; she loved France.

Life is a process of self-discovery.

Laura thrived in experiencing other cultures. One of the couples in our home fellowship group danced with Ballet Florida in West Palm Beach and the wife's home was in the southern part of England. We arranged for Laura to spend an additional week at our friend's home, hosted by her parents. They welcomed Laura warmly and she quickly discovered that English pubs were significantly different than American bars; they encouraged family patronage. Laura was fast becoming a seasoned world traveler, while Janet and I remained homebound.

With Laura away in college, Julie decided to leave her job at the hotel and take a job at an Old Navy store in Atlanta in the summer of 1994. Julie's best friend from TKA, Jamie, had moved there with her mom and she and Julie planned to become roommates. It was short-lived, however, since Jamie met a guy, fell in love and married him. Julie was alone, but remained in Atlanta.

Changes occurred on the home front as well. Larry Lambert heard the call of God to leave Fountain of Life Church and hit the road as an evangelist. This was neither easy, nor comfortable, leaving the 'security' of the church he and Elaine founded, but the alternative was worse. *It's never good to disobey God's call*—think of Jonah and the whale. He and Elaine finally left, but not before establishing his son-in-law and daughter as pastors to take over Fountain of Life.

Clearly, Janet was no longer dependent on the Lamberts for their ministry, and by early spring of 1995, it became apparent that it was time for us to move on as well. Moving on was often agonizing with severed friendships, but this time it was for a different reason. We experienced discord with some of the church leaders. Our closest friends, those from our home group and a few others, left with us.

I was intrigued that we were seven years at Nativity Lutheran where we experienced Cursillo and blossomed as new believers. We were seven years at Maranatha where we sat under a gifted teacher and devoured our Bibles as our handbook of life. We were seven years at Fountain of Life where we were saturated in the things of the Spirit and learned to hear from God ourselves. The Lord prepared us for something; what did He plan for us now?

Immediately, a group of us began to meet in our home with Mike Maass as our pastor. Mike was the music minister at Fountain of Life and, over the past several years, we developed a close friendship. Mike was not only extremely bright, but also sensitive to the Spirit. He was raised in Palm Beach and, along with another Palm Beach couple, we eventually established our new church as Palm Beach Christian Fellowship. Mike was president and, once again, I became vice president.

I don't know how she heard about us, but a woman living in Ft. Lauderdale began attending our church in Palm Beach. Every Sunday, she would drive that distance simply to hear Mike's spirit-inspired messages. That's how Janet and I met and befriended Alice Basham, a minister's widow. Coincidentally, I had read my first book on spiritual warfare years earlier, *Deliver Us From Evil*, authored by her deceased husband, Don Basham.

While alive, Don Basham regularly met with a group of ministers in Ft. Lauderdale to ponder spiritual matters. Derek Prince, a world-renowned theologian from England, was part of that group. In the late 1990s Janet and I joined Alice at a church in Ft. Lauderdale where Derek Prince was speaking and, afterwards, she graciously introduced us to him. That was awesome.

Later in the spring of 1995, Mike Maass and I attended my first (and only) Promise Keepers rally at the Orange Bowl in Miami hosted by a pastor named Joseph Garlington. While it was a good experience, I had heard many of the lessons previously. Larry Lambert often taught that husbands ought to love their wives as Christ loved the church (Ephesians 5:25), fathers not to provoke my children to anger (Ephesians 6:4), and simply to keep promises—"...let your 'Yes' be 'Yes,' and your 'No,' 'No.'" (Matthew 5:37).

Somehow, during conversations with Alice, she mentioned that she and Don were friends with Joseph Garlington. Imagine our surprise when years later, while visiting Janet's home in Wilkinsburg, we went to a church only one mile away and the pastor was Joseph Garlington. After that Sunday service, we just had to tell him that we had a mutual friend, Alice Basham. He smiled. We do live in a small world.

Because of my friendship with Mike Maass, I sponsored him to a Cursillo (re-named Via de Cristo) and, on that Saturday, Janet and I participated in some of the weekend activities. We returned home late that night and being hungry stopped at a fast food establishment on US-1 where I ordered food. Unexpectedly, the Holy Spirit whispered to me clearly and said, *"He didn't wash his hands!"* I knew exactly what that meant. The person who took our order and was preparing our food did so with bare hands, his unsanitary bare hands. *I knew that God was telling me to cancel the order and walk away.*

Immediately, I was conflicted. I did not want to confront that person and cancel our order even though I just heard directly from the Spirit. Instead, I bought the food, Janet and I ate it and we drove home.

There is no up-side to flagrantly disobeying God, particularly when He speaks directly to a person. The Bible even says, *"Behold, to obey is better than sacrifice"* (1 Sam.15:22). He was very displeased with me...how did I know? He took me to the woodshed. *"For whom the Lord loveth He chasteneth..."* (Heb. 12:6a). About 3:00 AM that morning, I woke up with one splitting headache—like the pounding of a stake being driven through my head. It was the worst headache since my brain tumor in 1979. I feared for my life and immediately repented for my disobedience. After about twenty minutes of intense repenting, the excruciating pain subsided and, I believe, was forgiven.

Janet, meanwhile, slept soundly next to me, oblivious to the crisis I had just encountered. Obviously, I was still learning.

Mike Maass was sensitive to the Spirit and effectively ministered to other people. Over a period of time, Janet began the second phase of her healing of sexual abuse with Mike and Donna (one of Janet's friends) praying for her. While this period was not as intense as the time spent with the Lamberts, it still lasted a couple of years. However, that's Janet's story and not mine.

29
VACATION CRISIS

D URING THE SUMMER of 1995, Janet and I took Laura and Peter to visit Julie in Atlanta. At this time Julie lived alone in a small apartment, and we crashed her solitude. We've always been a close family and what better way to create strong family ties than vacation together? One of the events Julie planned was a little whitewater rafting on the Chattahoochee River in Atlanta. I remember the day, July 20, 1995, because it was the 26th anniversary of Neil Armstrong's "One small step for man; one giant leap for mankind"—the first moon walk by the astronauts.

I'm casual about most things and never gave a second thought that I just signed a waiver absolving the raft company should anything go wrong. What was the company not telling me?

As we began our rafting adventure, the Chattahoochee River was probably flowing about two miles per hour. We had the most leisurely time floating past beautiful homes and taking in the scenery. I was sitting on the back of the raft while Janet and the others were sitting on the sides. On the bottom of the raft there was a life jacket for each of us, but that's where they remained. After about an hour-and-a-half, Janet heard what sounded like a highway in the distance, only it wasn't a highway, but the beginning of the rapids. Finally! That's why we took this ride—a little whitewater rafting adventure.

The rapids were rated between 2–3 on a scale of 5 and we were all looking forward to some excitement. Julie had gone to a college in Tennessee, and for the Atlanta Olympics, the Olympic Committee selected a river near Julie's college for the kayaking competition. That's a river I avoided; the Chattahoochee was more my speed.

When we reached the rapids, Janet immediately slid down to the bottom of the raft and within minutes it got hung up on a boulder near the surface. While Janet was shrieking excitedly, I was having a ball. Eventually, we dislodged our raft from the boulder and began to head downstream when the unexpected happened. While sitting securely on the back of the raft, somehow, my center of gravity shifted and I began to fall backwards.

"Oh no!" Desperately, I tried to grab onto something, but there was only air. I hit the water flush with my back and sank like a dead weight.

My first reaction while underwater was to reach for my glasses and with a finger hold them onto my nose, while my second reaction was to fill my lungs with air. I saw light above me, kicked vigorously with my legs and quickly broke the surface of the water, sucking in as much air as possible.

Immediately, that mishap became even more dramatic. Laura, who loves me dearly (actually they all do), dove into the water to rescue me, only we weren't even close; we never even touched pinkies as we were flopping about. I yelled to Janet to throw the life preserver from the raft and she threw it, but it tangled with some rope and never came close to either of us. The screams now were genuine.

I was being swept downstream while vigorously fighting the current and remember thinking, *"I do not want to drown with my family watching."* Being rescued, however, looked improbable. The far bank was a 150 feet away and reaching it would be impossible. The near bank was only 30 feet away, except the current was so swift, it may as well have been 100 feet. I could not reach either bank. The current continued taking me further downstream, away from my family, the raft, and safety.

Janet, Julie, and Peter had a dreadful decision to make…who to rescue first? That decision became evident since Laura remained closer to the raft, while I was being swept downstream. I can't explain that. Laura became top priority. It took several minutes to finally get her back into the raft—at one point they pulled her by her hair, along with that wayward life preserver and one of the paddles which had also fallen into the water.

By now, even though I had only been in the water for minutes, I was getting fatigued and losing strength. How much longer could I swim against the current, keep my head above water and avoid being swept downstream even further? I did not want to lose sight of my family…*I did not want to drown!*

In desperation, I yelled to Peter to bring the raft; he was about 50 feet away. With Laura safely on the raft, he vigorously paddled towards me. Finally, when the raft reached me, I quickly slipped my finger through a metal ring on the bow and relaxed every muscle in my body. I was safe. I avoided drowning, but that was far too close for comfort. *I just survived my harrowing experience number four!*

A few minutes after the family got me safely on board, we paddled to a clearing on the shoreline, beached the raft, got out and simply thanked

God for saving my life. The five of us had a rather emotional moment. Then, we asked another person who was there to take a picture of us to immortalize the event. That photo turned out so well that we used it for our Christmas card in 1995, and have it hanging on our family room wall to this day.

I faced two critical dangers that day. Obviously, the first was that of drowning, but the second was hitting any rocks or boulders in the river, which is how we got hung up in the first place. Sometimes, I remember how Christopher Reeve became paralyzed by falling off a horse and breaking his neck. Smashing my head, neck or spine on a boulder underwater may have had the same effect on me. I could have easily been paralyzed.

That morning, however, Janet had read Psalm 18:16, "*...he drew me out of many waters*" and Psalm 91:12, "*...lest thou dash thy foot against a stone.*" Merely hours earlier, Janet had read about God protecting somebody from drowning and hitting rocks, the exact two dangers I faced. Yet, I never swallowed a drop of water or even touched a rock. That photo hanging on our family room wall is a memorial to God sparing my life on the Chattahoochee River that July 20th.

One may wonder why my first reaction underwater was not to breathe, but to secure my glasses on my head. Several years earlier, I had taken Peter on a Father-Son canoe trip with a group from church; it was an eight-mile trek meandering through Jonathan Dickinson State Park, where we often had church picnics.

As we started out on our canoe adventure, we drifted too close to the bank and a branch from a tree literally picked the glasses off my head and were simply dangling there, teasing me to retrieve them. With my hand merely inches away from reaching my glasses, the branch seemingly let go of them and they dropped into the water.

The water was inky black and I had no idea how deep it was or if there were any gators lurking nearby. Since one of the lenses was already scratched, I decided to say 'adios' to those glasses, which became problematic. Without corrective lenses, my vision is worse than 20/200 as I cannot see the big 'E' on an eye chart. For the next eight miles everything I saw was severely out of focus.

On the Chattahoochee River that day, I did not want to lose another pair of glasses.

At one point on that Father-Son canoe trip, we had to literally lift our canoe over a fallen tree branch in the water. It was perilous and, not surprisingly, Peter slipped and fell into the water. Before the current could sweep him downstream, however, I jumped into the water, put my arm around his waist and held him close to me. I had to save my son. The water was still inky black and there may have been gators nearby, but I was highly motivated. Peter reciprocated that day on the Chattahoochee River when he brought the raft to save me.

At another point in our canoe adventure, there was an old fashioned swimming hole and about thirty fathers and sons took a break in canoeing and frolicked in the water just like Tom Sawyer or Huckleberry Finn would have done. We had a blast, even though I couldn't see anything underwater, but heck, I could barely see anything above water anyway. Sadly, about three weeks later, a little boy was killed by an alligator in the same area. What were we thinking?

One of the ironies in my life is that the one requirement that almost prevented me from graduating from Columbia was passing a swimming test. Columbia believed that by knowing how to swim, one could prevent a drowning. I can't dispute that logic. I've been athletic my entire life, but never learned how to swim because of frequent ear infections. I avoided taking that mandated swimming test at Columbia for nearly four years.

Finally, about one month before graduation, I got busted! The administration sent me a letter reminding me to take the swimming test or else I would not graduate. Dutifully, I trudged to the university swimming pool where the head basketball coach was there to monitor my test. I had taken a gym class with him years earlier and he certainly knew I was athletic, but could I swim? I only had to swim three laps of the pool, 25 yards per lap, and did my own personal medley...a little freestyle, backstroke, side stroke, doggy paddle...anything to complete those laps. I certainly won no style points, but churned through those three laps and passed the test. In reality, I learned to swim at our pool in North Palm Beach, and that's what saved my life on the Chattahoochee River that day.

30
MY FAMILY MIGRATES SOUTH

BECAUSE OF AN unexpected and traumatic divorce, my brother George moved to Florida in the fall of 1984. Linda, his ex, phoned me and encouraged us to take in George since he had no good place to go. It would have been too painful to remain near his former wife with all their shared memories and returning to Bridgeport was not an option. George and I had always gotten along well as he was an outstanding big brother. Janet and I opened our home to him. It was crowded before George arrived, but we all adjusted. He was a trooper and stayed only a couple months. In time, he met a lovely lady, married her and moved out.

I was always grateful that I grew to be 6'2" and George was 6'5", while my dad was a muscular 5'7". At Columbia, I learned that the 'tall' gene is dominant and my mom was 5'8," tall for a woman of her age. Nobody ever hassled me growing up because I had a giant of a brother nearby.

George became an avid golfer and, in 1990, while swinging his golf club, felt a painful twinge in his back. He went to a doctor and ultimately was diagnosed with multiple myeloma—a cancer of the bone marrow. (He had smoked much of his life.) Because of his cancer and the uncertainty of his remaining time, he strongly encouraged our parents to move south.

After living in same home in Connecticut for 55 years, my parents (both in their eighties) moved to South Florida in the autumn of 1996. George's three children and ex-wife helped my parents move; it was nearly overwhelming. Janet found them a first floor condominium in an adult community only three miles from us and there was a little Lutheran church within walking distance. It was perfect for them. George spent quality time with Mom at least once a week, while Dad was stricken with Alzheimer's.

In anticipation of Laura's college graduation in 1997, Julie also transferred to an Old Navy store in West Palm Beach and moved home, since she and Laura are the best of friends. Suddenly, our home became busy with activity. Laura taught kindergarten at The King's Academy and, for the next academic year, carpooled with her mom, still a third grade teacher, and Peter, a junior in high school. Once again, we were just one big, happy family living together. How long would that last? Not for long!

Less than a year of teaching at TKA, Laura heard the siren call of Europe beckoning. In the spring of 1998, one of her professors at Southeastern who knew that Laura had the heart of a missionary offered her a position as a missionary-teacher at an English-speaking church-school in Brussels, Belgium. Laura jumped at the offer.

I asked Laura how much she would be paid and thought that was a perfectly reasonable question, but she quickly reminded me that, as a missionary, we would need to support her. Not again! Laura, however, is extremely gregarious and was able to solicit financial support from many friends. Even Mike Maass (through Palm Beach Christian Fellowship) contributed to Laura's missionary fund.

For our 30th wedding anniversary in 1998, Janet and I planned a bold adventure; we booked our third cruise, a seven day 'Inside Passage' fare to Alaska. We discovered the enormous appeal of traveling from the extreme southeastern tip of the nation where it's sunny, flat, and hot, to the extreme northwest, where it's cloudy, mountainous, and cool.

Janet and I had a fabulous time. We took our first-ever helicopter ride to walk on a glacier...being mindful not to fall into any of the crevices, cruised Glacier Bay to hear the tidal glaciers calving...breaking off into the bay with the sound of a gunshot, visited the riotous Red Dog Saloon in the land-locked capital of Juneau, and in Ketchikan took a train ride which followed the path of the gold rush prospectors of the mid-1800s. As the train chugged up the side of the mountain, the vistas were breathtaking although I purposely never looked down.

Our fondest memory was meeting a fellow passenger who had three sons...a doctor, a lawyer and a missionary. This dad was so proud of his doctor and lawyer sons, but merely shook his head despondently while talking about his third son, the missionary. Janet and I simply couldn't contain ourselves. We told him how our own daughter was becoming a missionary and that his third son was likely following the call of God in his life. There was no higher calling; the man wept.

Upon returning home from our joyful anniversary cruise, Julie picked us up at the airport and immediately burst our bubble. Both of my parents were in the hospital, different ones at that. My dad had developed a blood infection and while he was being admitted to the Jupiter Medical Center, Julie insisted a nurse check out my mom who was very pale and clammy. Mom's heart was pumping at five percent and was close to death. Events happened quickly. She was transported to the Palm Beach Gardens Medical Center, noted for their cardiology unit, and had a triple by-pass heart surgery at age 83. Julie just saved my mom's life. Both my parents recovered.

Sadly, George was not doing well. For most of his adult life he weighed about 250 pounds, but the summer and fall of 1998, he kept losing weight. Our birthdays are only 13 days apart in August and when he and his wife visited Janet and me for a combined party, George spoke with me privately. He knew his days were numbered and asked me to pray for his wife and his three children. To honor his request I've included George's family in my daily prayers ever since that birthday celebration.

George and I always had a brotherly love for each other, but our personal theologies were dramatically different. From the beginning of our marriage, Janet and I not only attended church, but got involved and surrounded ourselves with church friends. George, however, rarely went to church, nor did he encourage his family to go. Yet, personally, he felt he had a close relationship with God and frequently heard His voice.

Sadly, George passed away on Monday, December 1, 1998, merely four days after he and his wife had a wonderful Thanksgiving dinner at our home with my family and our parents. After eight years of fighting courageously, he finally succumbed to the multiple myeloma. We miss him.

Larry Lambert taught me that as a husband and father, I was the priest of my family and as priest it was my spiritual responsibility to pray for them daily. I've accepted my role and, since 1986, have prayed for my family (including George's widow and children) and friends the following: (1) protection of people, (2) purity, (3) protection of property, (4) spiritual warfare, (5) wisdom, (6) blessings, and (7) salvation of others. My family depends on me for that daily prayer.

31
BLESSINGS AND TROUBLES

BURSTING WITH FAITH and optimism, our dear Laura embarked on the adventure of her young life by moving to Europe. As the wheels of her aircraft touched down in Brussels, her life as a missionary-teacher began. How did she ever manage to carry those two packed duffel bags and carry-on luggage filled with essentials? It was early October, 1998, and she shared an apartment with two roommates in Waterloo, a suburb of Brussels made famous by Napoleon.

One of her favorite activities was visiting the Grand Plaz and soaking up the Belgian culture as well as tasting its famed chocolate morsels. She studied to speak French fluently, one of the languages spoken there and although on a limited budget, still managed to visit countries surrounding Belgium. Occasionally, she drove to Antwerp with church friends to witness to prostitutes.

That December, a friend introduced me to someone who wanted to renovate a master bath and outdoor roof deck of her townhouse. Because of the size of the project and our improving financial situation, I offered my services to my new client not only as an architect, but also a contractor. Once she agreed, I began the process of activating my general contractor's license and incorporating as a business.

The attorney who discovered the glitch in the plat ten years earlier prepared the documents for incorporation and when he researched the name 'Creative Custom Design' prophesied by Gary Brooks in 1994, he was pleased to inform me it was still available. It took nearly three months, but in early 1999, I finally became a licensed GC operating as Creative Custom Designs, Inc.

The project proceeded well, although it took longer than expected, no surprise there. Often, there is a positive ripple effect with any construction activity and that happened to me. Others in the same community wanted similar work done and I was pleased to oblige.

During spring break of 1999, Janet and I finally leaped that insurmountable hurdle...we traveled to Europe! We just had to see Laura. Frequent flier miles took care of our flight and we lodged with Laura while in Brussels before taking side trips.

The first was to Bruges where we climbed to the top of the Bell Tower in the middle of the town square, all 365 stairs. Janet's knees punished her for that climb. Next, we traveled east to Harlem, Netherlands, and toured Corrie ten Boom's 'Hiding Place'—where her family hid Jews during World War II—visited the Keukenhof Gardens with its acres of flowers and spent one night in Amsterdam before returning to Waterloo. Of course, Laura showed us the Gran Plaz and its Mannequin Pis.

Our highlight was taking the high speed train from Brussels to Paris to experience the City of Lights. Why were so many people flocking to the cathedral of Notre Dame? It was Good Friday - duh! We dined at a Paris café in the shadow of the Eiffel Tower before enduring those queues to ascend to the observation deck and enjoy its stunning view. While strolling along the Champs Elysees, we ate our ice cream cones before reaching the Arc d'Triumph and climbed those 256 steps to the top which, once again, aggravated Janet's knees. With time running out we made a mad dash through the Louvre to view Da Vinci's *Mona Lisa* and were surprised how small it was, and, yes, we took a boat ride on the Seine River. Our first visit to Europe just became a treasured memory.

That spring Peter graduated from The King's Academy along with 90 classmates, and we expected him to follow the lead of Julie and Laura who attended small Christian colleges. Peter thought differently; he applied to University of Florida with its 45,000 students. Our son was about to get devoured! He and his best friend, Judd, expected to be roommates while Janet and I were clueless, but acquiesced to his decision.

Sometime in April or early May I telephoned the admissions office at UF to check on Peter's status and learned that he was still on the waiting list. That was disappointing. The administrator then mentioned that because of the crowded housing conditions, each undergraduate would be required to spend at least one summer semester on campus. I replied that that would be no problem for Peter and then she asked if Peter would be willing to spend his first semester on campus for the upcoming summer session. I said, "Yes." Immediately, she said Peter was accepted and he became a 'Gator!' Unexpectedly, Judd was not accepted to UF.

Meanwhile, disaster struck on Tuesday, May 13, 1999.

While working on my first construction project, I was climbing to the top of a six-foot-high rolling scaffold when it began to topple over. My client had hired painters and their truck was parked exactly where the scaffold was falling. Within a nanosecond my mind assessed the situation, and, not wanting to pay for a damaged vehicle, I pushed off the scaffold with my legs in the opposite direction of the fall and, miraculously, the scaffold tottered, but never fell. However, I did! I crash landed stiff-legged on the concrete driveway which sent shock waves of excruciating pain up my spine. I remained curled up on the driveway fearing even to move, the whole time wondering if I was paralyzed.

Ever so slowly, I managed to stand up and to my surprise my back supported me and was even able to walk a few baby steps. I entered the townhouse, lay down on a sofa, and prayed fervently for healing; I was desperate. I could not afford to be disabled and out of work. The Lord had always protected me from any serious injury, even death, but what just happened was potentially devastating.

For hours I lay there praying that my back was not seriously injured. I told the painters about my accident and asked if they would disassemble the scaffold and load it into my SUV, so that I could return it that afternoon on time. I then drove to the scaffold rental office and was thankful that the seat in my SUV was so comforting on my back.

Then, I did a smart thing by driving to the Emergency Room at the Jupiter Medical Center for X-rays on my back. After reviewing the X-rays, the emergency room doctor apparently thought I was well enough to release me and I drove home.

With the fall I could have shattered any number of vertebrae, which would have crippled me or even severed my spine, possibly resulting in death, but my spine remained intact. That was an answer to prayer, and I was able to work.

My experience wasn't over, however. The next day I received a phone call from the Jupiter Medical Center and the caller said an orthopedic surgeon reviewed my X-rays and wanted me to return to the JMC to have an MRI taken of my back, which I did.

One thought really unnerved me. One day earlier, I had erected that scaffold to its full height—about eleven to twelve feet high and climbed to the top to work on the second floor eave. I felt very uneasy with my head approximately eighteen feet above that concrete driveway on a rather shaky scaffold and after a few moments had the good sense to descend safely. Had I fallen off the scaffold at that height, I may not have survived.

That weekend, May 17–18, 1999, was Peter's University of Florida "Preview

Weekend," his indoctrination into a student's life at UF. Needless to say, that was a terrible time for me, but Janet and I drove him to Gainesville. I was impressed with the campus. The weekend itself was non-stop for Peter, rushing from one activity to another, but he was young, energetic and excited about college life. I was the parent—been there, done that— and my aching back limited my activities.

Before beginning our trip home on Monday morning, we stopped at a fast food place and each of us had a sandwich, beverage, and chocolate chip cookies. The trip home would have been uneventful except for one thing—sugar.

Over the years whenever my family took a road trip, I often became drowsy while driving on an interstate. One time while driving south on I-95, I became so drowsy that my eyelids felt like 100-pound weights, and I struggled to keep them open even though it was only mid-morning. What was happening? Somehow, I deduced that I had a touch of hypoglycemia, and the combination of sugar circulating through my bloodstream while driving on a superhighway at high speeds was potentially lethal for me. As a result, whenever my family made a road trip, I purposely avoided eating anything containing sugar so I would remain alert.

I forgot that precaution in Gainesville that morning and ate chocolate chip cookies, filled with sugar. While driving south on I-75, once again, I became drowsy. Janet was asleep beside me with Peter conked out in the back seat and it was only mid-morning…it was an exhausting weekend. I was following a panel truck about six car-lengths in front of me traveling at seventy-five miles per hour when it happened. *I fell asleep at the wheel of the car!*

With my head slumped down and right foot unwittingly pressing down on the accelerator, I was only seconds away from colliding with that panel truck. I can't explain it, but somehow, I jerked my head up, opened my eyes and immediately hit the brake. Playing bumper-cars traveling at now eighty miles an hour would not have been as benign as my favorite amuse- ment park ride. I just avoided wiping out not just me, but Janet and Peter as well. That was far too close for comfort, *"my harrowing experience number five!"*

After Peter's Preview Weekend I met with the orthopedic surgeon to discuss the results of the MRI on my back. We quickly discovered that we shared common ground; he graduated from Columbia's Medical School. We chatted about the merits of Columbia's football coaches over the years.

Then he got down to the business as he said, "John, your back is a mess, not because of the two cracked vertebrae meaning, technically, *you have a broken back*, but you have a congenital condition called Stenosis along with some arthritis."

The openings behind my vertebrae enclosing my spinal cord—containing the nerves from brain stem to legs—were literally too small for my frame and the arthritis was further exasperating this condition. The nerves to my legs were being constricted affecting the muscles in my calves. He cautioned me that if I experienced any tingling in my legs, I should sit to relieve pressure in my back. The tingling never occurred. I asked him whether exercise would alleviate the Stenosis; he said "No." Essentially, I would need to live with this condition.

The cracked vertebrae healed, but the Stenosis was ever present. I had felt the effects for the first time in 1987 while pitching baseballs to my six-year-old son, when I felt a painful twinge in my back. At the time I was baffled about that twinge, but discovered the cause 12 years later.

32
ROUND TWO

PETER GRADUATED FROM TKA in the spring of 1999, and missed his summer vacation to enroll at UF. After 11 years of teaching at TKA, Janet retired for the second time and became that stay-at-home mom she had always desired. But now, only Julie remained at home and she didn't need mothering. Laura thrived as a missionary-teacher and I was busy with a couple of small projects in the same community as my first construction project.

In early November Laura had her week-long holiday and Janet and Julie visited her in Brussels. Together, they traipsed off to see England and Scotland. It wasn't balmy. They spent the first few days in London before taking the train to the highlands of Scotland and spontaneously did a bold thing—they joined a backpacking tour. This tour was for younger people and the guide cleaned up his language when Janet arrived and everybody called her 'Mum.' She fit right in.

It was more perilous than expected with rain on the mountainous terrain, washed-out roads and being too close to a herd of easily-spooked hairy coos (cows). They saw Loch Ness, but not its famous monster, and bought a bottle of Scotch from the smallest distillery in Scotland. As Laura embraced France, Julie loved Scotland.

After returning home weeks before Thanksgiving, Janet declared, "I'm bored!" She said she always wanted to be that stay-at-home mom, but Laura and Peter were living elsewhere and only Julie lived at home and she read most of the time. Janet thrives on activity and there was none on the home front. The Lord apparently empathized with Janet's frustration because, once again, the phone rang! *The King's Academy telephoned Janet and asked her to return teaching a third grade class...again.* Talk about "déjà vu!"

TKA had just fired another third grade teacher in the middle of the year and, again, was desperate to find a quality teacher. That's the grade Janet had previously taught for 11 years at TKA and she said "yes."

By this time I asked a former architectural client to partner with me to build a spec home in River Ridge. He agreed to finance the project while I prepared the architectural drawings and did the construction. That was year 2000. I learned quickly that partnerships are not always the smoothest of relationships and that became my first and last partnership ever.

That August Peter was just beginning his sophomore year at UF when he created a chat room on the internet and connected with a freshman coed from UCLA. Peter and Diana quickly became an item. Communicating on the internet was free for Peter as I had paid for the family's internet service. Peter's grades were his best at UF since his girlfriend lived three thousand miles away and he wasn't dating at UF.

Peter had sent pictures of himself to Diana and Diana sent Peter her pictures. She was gorgeous and thin. By Christmastime we encouraged Peter to invite Diana to visit us in Florida, but she said her twin brother was involved in an automobile accident and she simply couldn't leave. We prayed for her brother.

In February, 2001, I got an unexpected jolt—Peter's cell phone bill was over $500.00. Apparently, communicating on the internet for Peter and Diana became secondary to actually talking by phone. I was livid.

Yet, Peter was so emotionally involved with Diana that I needed to handle this situation delicately. I did not want to crush my son.

It was time to meet Diana.

Peter knew I was angry with his cell phone bill, but when I suggested that he and I fly to Los Angeles and meet Diana face to face during his upcoming spring break, he was all smiles. My reasoning was that if Peter and Diana were meant to be together, they need to find out now or otherwise end it. Peter made the arrangements with Diana for our visit.

In March 2001, during Peter's spring break, he and I flew to Los Angeles to meet the love of his life. Our flight touched down at LAX (L.A.'s airport) on a Friday evening. We picked up our red Mustang convertible I had rented for the weekend and checked into our motel room nearby. Seven months after connecting in that chat room, Peter would finally meet his Diana. They had arranged to meet at Diana's townhouse in L.A. and on that Saturday morning I drove Peter to their long-anticipated meeting.

While I remained in the car, Peter walked to her townhouse alone. When Diana opened the door, Peter got the shock of his life. Their relationship was *one big, fat lie.* Diana was not a freshman at UCLA, but a junior in high school; she was a mixed child, her mother was an African-American doctor; she had no twin brother, she was an only child; the pictures she sent were of her gorgeous, thin cousin (but who knows), although she did include a baby picture of herself; she was certainly not thin as she weighed 184 pounds.

Peter was devastated. He walked back to me in the Mustang projecting sadness upon sadness and simply said, "Dad, pray for me..."

Peter, however, is one remarkable person. Despite his utter shock and disappointment, he spent that entire Saturday with Diana going to a school function in San Diego with her high school classmates. That evening he insisted on meeting Diana's mother and explain to her that any relationship based on a lie would never succeed, and theirs was based on a lie. I, likely, would not have done that.

Sunday we just hung out. We rode around Hollywood with the top down and the heat on since it was chilly, toured Rodeo Drive and the beaches before going to a movie.

As we left the motel for our flight home Monday morning, Peter asked if we could get a piece of pie at a nearby Denny's Restaurant. At that point I wasn't about to deny Peter anything. We went to the Denny's and sat at the counter to save time and ordered our pie.

Sitting next to me was a young lady and we started talking. She asked the obvious question, "What are you doing in L.A.?" I told her about Peter's internet romance that went south and she laughed. Peter and I merely stared, drained of emotion.

She then asked Peter the most bizarre question, "Do you have a summer job?" Peter mumbled something and she continued by explaining she worked for Southwestern Publishing, a company founded in 1868, that originally sold Bibles door to door, but now sold educational books to families with children. Southwestern hired college students to sell during a thirteen-week summer program and she asked if Peter would be interested. "Yes." She then told Peter she would contact the representative at the University of Florida. Peter wrote down his name and telephone number at UF, gave her the information and by this time we had to dash to catch our flight.

As we left Denny's, I told Peter that if anything came of this encounter, it had to be God...and it was. The Southwestern rep at UF did contact Peter, the company trained him in sales and for the next two summers he sold their products door to door. He was mildly successful, but his training and experience have been invaluable to this day, all because of a "chance" encounter at a Denny's lunch counter 3000 miles away after a failed internet romance.

Here's the proverbial icing on the cake; that young lady at the lunch counter was Kyah Grady, the top salesperson at Southwestern Publishing at that time. She was the one who set the bar for sales, and she was the one who just recruited Peter. Who could have written a better Hollywood script for jump-starting Peter's career?

33
FAMILY TIME

LAURA WAS A missionary-teacher in Brussels for two years, but the third year she taught at a private English-speaking international school, salary included. Yes! After living there nearly three years, Laura was planning to return home the summer of 2001. Janet and I just had to visit her one final time and scheduled our trip during Janet's spring break.

Our flight touched down in Brussels on Friday, March 16, and Laura took us to her school to meet friends and faculty. They were celebrating St. Patrick's Day one day early as her headmistress was Irish. Although we were jet-lagged, the festivities rejuvenated us.

As Laura's spring break was still weeks away, she had to teach the following week giving Janet and me the opportunity to visit London for a few days. I wanted to see buildings and sites I had studied while taking art history courses at Columbia.

By Thursday evening Laura finished teaching for the week and the three of us began our own version of a "Tour d' France." We drove to Rouen (to see where Joan of Arc was burned at the stake), saw the nearly 1000-year-old Bayou Tapestry (commemorating William the Conqueror's invasion of England in 1066), walked Omaha Beach and the World War II Memorials (I'm a WWII buff), spent the night at Mont Saint-Michel (an eighth century monastery built on an enormous rock on the shore of the North Sea), traveled through the fields of Normandy on our way to see the famous castles along the Loire Valley. We toured the magnificent medieval cathedral at Chatres before driving around Paris and returned to Brussels Sunday evening. Laura did all the driving, a one thousand mile jaunt over three plus days, and we made grand memories.

My favorite was our greeting at Chartres Cathedral. As we entered, displayed directly in front of us, was the Shroud of Turin. Many people believe the Shroud to be the actual burial cloth of Jesus Christ. Since I'm a believer, seeing the Shroud was like discovering a long lost treasure. It was protected by a thick plexiglass case and Laura took photos of it. Of course, it may have been a replica, but I was still awe-struck. The Lord delights in surprises.

It should be mentioned that before our long drive, we stopped at a large discount store in Brussels to stock up on Belgian chocolate, coffee and other treats for our return trip to the States as there would be no time to shop after our road trip. The dad of one of my college roommates commented, "The road to hell is paved with good intentions!"

As we left Mont Saint-Michel and drove through those lush, green fields of Normandy listening to an Enya CD, Laura detected the aroma of potato chips wafting from the back seat. Janet had opened one bag of chips, but in reality just opened the floodgates. That Belgian chocolate never had a chance. The three of us devoured the entire chocolate booty as we drove! Of course, we were all giddy on a sugar high, and I was grateful Laura drove.

After returning home that June, Laura was hired by The King's Academy to teach kindergarten. She and Julie were living at home once again after each had moved away for three years. They certainly qualify as 'boomerang kids,' those who leave home only to return. Janet and I loved it.

Peter worked for Southwestern selling educational materials the summer of 2001. All those college kids were required to be independent and separated from family. Peter's sales area was Troy, Michigan, a suburb of Detroit. He became well acquainted with rejection—cold calling is never easy, but also was mildly successful through sheer perseverance by working over 80 hours a week.

At one of Peter's calls, he met a young pastor who instantly bonded with him. Both were similar theologically and very passionate about the things of God. He was convincing Peter to become his youth pastor and not return to UF. When Janet and I first heard about this, I thought it was joke, not to be taken seriously. Peter, however, thought otherwise; for him this was a life-changing decision. Once again, Janet and I had to do our own family damage control. We considered Peter's graduation from college non-negotiable.

Fortunately, that summer we had planned a family vacation at Lakeside, Ohio, on the shore of Lake Erie, a couple hours east of Detroit. That was Janet's summer vacation growing up and years earlier her family even owned a cottage there. Since we would be so close to Peter, we arranged to rendezvous with him and together meet with the young pastor. He, alone, was not going to decide our son's future.

On the appointed day Janet and I drove from Lakeside to Troy, met

Peter and followed him to the pastor's home. We quickly realized why Peter bonded with him as he was charismatic in the true sense of the word. However, we were still the parents and wanted our son to complete his undergraduate degree. What Peter did with his life after college would be his choice.

We were pleasantly surprised to learn the young pastor was familiar with Christian International (CI) and held the prophetic in high esteem. By the end of the evening we all agreed that I would take Peter to CI for a prophetic word. Would Peter become a youth pastor or continue as a college student? That was the question for the Lord to answer.

There was a limited window of opportunity for Peter even to be home after his 13-week selling program, let alone visit CI. Fortunately, on the only Friday available, I was able to make an appointment for Peter and together we took a flight from West Palm Beach to Pensacola and drove our rental car the 70 miles east to Santa Rosa Beach, where CI was located.

On Friday evenings CI hosted a prophetic presbytery in which people from anywhere in the world could sign up to receive a personal prophecy. There were several teams of 'prophets' ministering and everything was tape-recorded for that person's use. On several occasions Janet and I drove eight hours each way and were always edified by our personal prophecy; we listened to our tape repeatedly on our return trip.

After Peter got his word, I smiled. During his prophecy, 'education' was mentioned about six times while there was a profound silence about becoming a youth pastor. Peter had no conflict returning to UF his junior year.

Peter took off that spring semester, but remained on campus to concentrate on assembling his Southwestern 'team' for the summer of 2002. Sadly, his efforts did not produce the anticipated windfall. Yet, that in itself was a valuable learning experience.

34
JOB BLESSINGS AND WOES

I N EARLY 2002, one of my neighbors commissioned me to design and build a bedroom suite for his mother who visited during the winter. The project was less than 300 square feet and progressed well.

Typically, as the contractor, I would oversee all my subcontractors and trades—plumbing, air conditioning, and electrical. For this project, however, my neighbor hired his own air conditioning contractor with whom he already had a relationship. I've always accommodated my clients even though such an arrangement may prolong the construction schedule.

Yet, everything worked out, or so I thought, until the owner received his invoice from the air conditioning contractor who charged him for extra work caused by "contractor delays." I was the contractor...how ironic.

My neighbor was upset and he blasted me. I defended myself as best as I could and we were squaring off for one legal tussle. Unfortunately for me, my neighbor's an attorney. I was agitated and knew sleep would elude me since I was emotionally agitated. Desperately, I prayed and turned the entire dispute over to the Lord. He could handle it far better than I and, believe it or not, I slept well that night.

The next day the most amazing thing happened. My neighbor phoned me and said he wanted to drop the whole dispute since we had always gotten along and he didn't want to create ill feelings between us. I believe the Lord, who is my greatest advocate, touched my neighbor's heart so that he changed his mind.

"It's not rocket science..." is an expression frequently heard in construction. The intent is obvious; contractors don't have to be nearly as exact as a rocket scientist to produce a successful project. Later that spring one of my clients *was* a rocket scientist. He planned to renovate his master bedroom suite by enlarging it and wanted a detached three car garage with a large playroom above. The project itself went well although he discerned even the slightest of flaws. We had met nearly twenty five years earlier since he and his wife also attended a Cursillo, although in a different movement.

Recently, he had surgery for an inguinal hernia and told me how he researched who would be the best doctor and which would be the best hospital for that particular surgery. In other words he did his 'due diligence.' Surgery went well for him and he was pleased.

At precisely the same time, I, too, had an inguinal hernia and the pain flared up announcing it was time for surgery. Did I research who would be my surgeon and where it would be done? Noooo! My 'due diligence' was to follow the script of my client, the rocket scientist. I couldn't improve on what he had done so I used the same doctor at the same hospital with the same result; surgery went well for me, too. The Lord's timing, once again, was impeccable.

In August 2002, Janet was just beginning her 15th year teaching third grade at The King's Academy. For the first 14 years she felt like the proverbial round peg trying to fit into a square opening, somewhat of a misfit. Janet had always been flamboyant while TKA was rigid—rules, rules, and more rules. You know who won that battle. Her students, however, absolutely adored Janet and told her in so many ways. One of her third grade students even penned the following poem:

> "Mrs. Nossal makes learning fun.
> During the year we learned a ton!
> She makes school exciting every day.
> How great she is words can not say.
> Bible is the subject I love the best.
> Thanks to her I can like the rest.
> I'll be in school for many a year,
> But I'll remember 3rd as especially dear.
> For the first time I'm sorry to see a year end.
> It's because I miss you, a special friend!"

That year Janet figuratively 'surrendered' to being at TKA. If the Lord wanted her to teach there until she died, she would be content with that. She never felt that way before.

That's when she got blindsided!

That fall her evaluation by her principal was not good; Janet needed to improve. The evaluations for the previous 14 years were nearly perfect; she needed to improve only on administrative details, not Janet's strong suit. But now, she needed to improve in other areas as well.

She met her principal to review the evaluation and he was adamant about her performance needing to improve. With over 25 years of teaching experience, Janet was one of their highest paid teachers and we wondered if that was a factor. She already taught 35 children in a small classroom for nearly 15 years. Thirty-five sets of grades for many subjects per week, and yet, she needed to improve.

We saw the writing on the wall; Janet was being pushed out. She felt betrayed and was devastated. This was especially hard to accept since Janet bailed out TKA not once, but twice, in the middle of the school year, hardly best time to hire a quality teacher. It seemed that TKA had a short memory. Nevertheless, Janet decided to complete the academic year and then leave TKA permanently. The remainder of that school year was extremely difficult for Janet; she consistently gave her all and had no more to give.

One Saturday in January 2003, a woman that Janet barely knew phoned her and asked what church we were attending. That was one odd question. About two-and-a-half years earlier we left Palm Beach Christian Fellowship on amicable terms with Mike Maass and had been visiting local churches. The woman phoned Janet to recommend two local churches she thought we might enjoy.

The next morning Janet and I visited the church closer to home. As we entered the sanctuary, who should greet us but our friends Richard and Peggy Daniels, whom we hadn't seen in years. Janet's first words to Peggy, "I'm leaving The King's Academy and don't have a job." Peggy responded, *"I'll hire you!"* By this time she had become a principal in one of the county schools and had wanted to work with Janet for the past 20 years. Apparently, it was now time.

Peggy walked her through the entire hiring process and Janet, once again, would be an elementary teacher in the county's school system for the next academic year. She was wise to maintain her Florida Teacher's Certificate through a series of courses every five years and was rewarded for her diligence. Janet was offered a salary 50 percent greater than what she was earning at TKA. We were surprised and overwhelmed with gratitude for the Lord.

For our 35th wedding anniversary that spring, Janet and I booked a 14-day "European Capitals Cruise" on a Holland America ship starting in Rome and ending in Copenhagen. We needed permission from TKA for Janet to leave a couple days early from the teachers' final work days although the students had already begun their summer vacation. At a faculty meeting on her final day at TKA, one of the administrators announced the "politically correct" news that Janet was retiring (rather than being pushed out), but what really delighted her was winning the school raffle for teachers and staff (with about 80 people attending). She felt that by winning the raffle God was validating her in everybody's presence. She cherished that.

What about Laura? She was still a kindergarten teacher at TKA under the same principal who insisted her mom improve after 25 years of teaching. Janet intuitively felt that Laura's days at TKA were numbered, but didn't know the number.

In early June Janet and I took our flight to Rome where we had booked a room only blocks from the famous Colosseum, which we never did visit. We spent two days site-seeing before embarking on our cruise.

After viewing Michelangelo's fabulous paintings of the Sistine Chapel, we began touring St. Peter's Square when, to Janet's surprise, she recognized familiar faces. Seniors from The King's Academy class trip just happened to be touring St. Peter's Square at exactly the same time as we were. Janet greeted them warmly. Years earlier she had many of these students in her third grade class. What an endearing final memory of TKA, a joyful encounter with students she had taught.

From my perspective, that 35th anniversary cruise was likely our best vacation ever. Often, Janet is so much fun to be with despite the trials and tragedies of her life. Larry Lambert once commented that when Janet's is 'on,' there was absolutely nobody like her. Her effervescence could not be contained, like an opened bottle of champagne with bubbles overflowing. When she's 'on,' she'll impishly ask somebody, "…What are the three things men like best?" After a brief silence, she'll answer her own question: "…Sex…Food…and Games!" Everybody laughs.

On that cruise, Janet's switch was 'on.' We were more amorous than ever, the food was superb, and I won playing bridge nearly every time, as well as visiting places we had only read about. Whenever he saw Janet, one of the sous chefs called her, 'Pretty Girl,' which she absolutely ate up. We just made another priceless memory.

Later that summer Janet, Julie and Laura, our family's version of the 'three amigos,' vacationed in Vancouver Island, British Columbia.

While working in my home office, I took a telephone call for Laura from the new principal of Palm Beach Public Elementary School, who was formerly Peggy Daniels' assistant principal. She asked Peggy for a recommendation to fill a kindergarten position and Peggy suggested Laura. I took the message and gave her Laura's cell phone number. She then phoned Laura, still vacationing in Canada, and they connected.

Janet's intuition about Laura leaving TKA happened much sooner than expected. After returning home from vacation, Laura was formally hired by the new principal, but needed to return to The King's Academy to retrieve some personal teaching supplies. While there, she met the same elementary principal who evaluated Janet nine months earlier and told him she took another job and would not be returning to TKA. Their meeting was not pleasant.

Palm Beach Public is an intriguing place. Julie, our first born, was tested 'gifted' prior to starting kindergarten. At that time Palm Beach Public had the only gifted kindergarten class in the county and since I worked in Palm Beach, I became Julie's car pool every morning. She attended about five years. If we were early enough I took Julie to a bakery, bought some cookies and drove to the beach to enjoy our treat with a magnificent view. Julie and I have many fond memories of Palm Beach Public and now Laura would be on its faculty. What a pleasant family connection.

35
JULIE'S JOB AND PETER'S WIFE

IN THE SUMMER of 2003, Peter took a couple courses at UF to complete his undergraduate requirements and graduated that August. We celebrated...how could we not? Our last child was through college. He moved home and, once again, we had a full house.

Janet began teaching at Peggy's school in West Palm Beach and I had secured a loan to build spec homes in St. Lucie County, forty five minutes north.

Janet, however, had a concern. Her oldest brother, Will, had congenital heart failure and she wondered about her own heart. She made an appointment with Dr. Vargas, my mom's cardiologist, and was pleased to discover that her heart was healthy. He advised her strongly, however, to stop taking hormones for HRT (hormone replacement therapy) which she had been taking since 1986. The HRT benefited her greatly although she had a tendency to gain weight. Nevertheless, new studies indicated HRT caused unacceptable health problems and under Dr. Vargas's orders, she stopped taking hormones.

Sadly, those demons of sexual abuse once again began to torment her. She had trouble sleeping and eventually stopped eating normally. Within a matter of months, she lost forty pounds...without dieting! I was alarmed not knowing when Janet would stop losing weight. Eventually, we both realized it was time for Janet to begin her third round of healing from sexual abuse.

Using her new school board insurance, she began to see a male psychologist who came highly recommended. After several weeks of counseling, however, Janet realized she was not getting anywhere and stopped seeing him.

Next, she began seeing a woman from a local church with a reputation for resolving sexual abuse issues in a group setting and Janet was intrigued. This woman assured Janet that in six weeks she would feel better. I thought to myself, "This will be interesting." Sadly, she underestimated the severity of Janet's problem and realized she would not be the one to help her.

Fortunately, this woman knew a psychologist named Catherine Moritz, and in May or June of 2004, introduced Janet to her. Catherine became the one who actually helped Janet.

Julie, meanwhile, has had an unusual work history. She had been a manager of an Old Navy store in Marietta, Georgia for three years before transferring to the West Palm Beach store as she wanted to be home when Laura graduated college in 1997. Julie is bright, highly organized and eventually achieved her goal of becoming the general manager of the Old Navy store in WPB.

There was only one problem; she hated retailing! The hours were endless, she was the one to deal with business mishaps (which were numerous), and she needed to resolve staff personnel problems. In July 1999, about a month after becoming the GM, Julie quit her job.

We were aware of Julie's intentions, so her quitting didn't surprise us, but what she did next surely did. She became a babysitter…for twins. To go from a GM to babysitting twins boggles the mind, but that was her choice.

She babysat for four years and had about 20 clients, all with twins. Finally, in late summer, 2003, she felt the urge to jump back into the work force and get a real job. Julie became a manager at one of the national book store chains, but quickly realized that the store was so poorly managed she didn't want to constantly put out fires and left after a couple months.

The Lord had graciously provided jobs, completely unsolicited, for everyone in our family except for her. She prayed and felt that He would provide a job for her, also unsolicited. Accordingly, she waited on the Lord. Janet and I were dubious about Julie's strategy and suggested she actively seek other employment. "… *Oh ye of little faith…* " (Matthew 16:8).

Then it happened!

In February, 2004, a woman who had seven-year-old twins telephoned Julie and asked if she would be interested in working for her, not as a babysitter, but as a personal assistant. The woman was friends with one of Julie's former clients with twins and that was the point of contact. Julie began her new career as a personal assistant and her responsibilities over the years have grown; it's been an extraordinary position.

Peter, meanwhile, had taken a couple sales jobs after graduating from

UF, but was getting nowhere. He applied to several law schools (even taking the LSAT) and divinity schools in the spring of 2004. The law schools didn't pan out, but he was accepted into the divinity program at Southeastern University in Lakeland, Florida, Laura's college.

However, Peter fell in love. He met an attractive young lady in our church and their relationship flourished. Peter is an incurable romantic and planned to propose to his girlfriend on her birthday, August 11th. He wooed her that entire day, making breakfast for her, taking her to the beach, treating her to lunch, paid for her massage, all before dinner. Throughout the day he gave her little presents, but was saving the best for last, the engagement ring after dinner.

As I was working in my home office that afternoon, I took a phone call from Regent University in Virginia Beach. The caller asked for Peter and I replied that he wasn't home, but as his dad, I would take a message. She informed me that Peter was accepted into their divinity program and asked whether or not he received his acceptance letter. He hadn't. To say I was surprised would be an understatement; I had no idea where Peter sent applications. Very clearly, however, I thought to myself that Peter was in love, he was about to propose to his girlfriend at dinnertime and he would not be going anywhere. Coincidentally, Peter's acceptance letter from Regent arrived that same afternoon.

Then, Peter's girlfriend broke up with him over dinner.

He wasn't about to marry after all. She spent the entire day with Peter receiving all the goodies he bought, including the massage, before ending their relationship.

Normally, I would have consoled Peter, but not this time. Instead, I told him that Regent University had telephoned to say that he was accepted into their divinity program and their acceptance letter arrived only hours earlier. Maybe, just maybe, the Lord was calling him to Regent.

Three weeks later, Peter was driving north to Virginia Beach to get a Master's degree in Divinity. What or perhaps who, did God have planned for Peter at Regent?

By this time I had completed and sold my first spec home in Port St. Lucie, which at that time was one of the fastest growing areas in the nation. The second spec home shared the same rear property line as the first although on the adjacent street. Both homes were three bedrooms, two baths, two-car garage homes with front and rear porches. They blended in with the neighborhoods.

I anticipated building in Port St. Lucie for the foreseeable future until the law of supply and demand finally kicked in. Lots that I had purchased for $20K–27K were now selling for $80K-$100K; I couldn't afford that. After selling the second home in the spring of 2005, I left Port St. Lucie and never looked back. Years later the real estate bubble burst with a ton of overpriced, unsold inventory, but I escaped unscathed.

In August of 2005, Julie and Laura took the bold step of purchasing a DiVosta four-plex in West Palm Beach and moved out of our home. They paid the market price, which was enormously inflated, but Julie had cash from the settlement of an automobile accident only a year earlier. Janet and I became empty nesters for the first time since 1970. I was content while Janet was mom, she missed them all.

Peter, meanwhile, spent two years at Regent and in the spring of 2006, graduated with his Master of Arts of Divinity. Not surprisingly, he met a female student at Regent, fell in love and this time married her. Interestingly, Melissa's home is Pittsburgh, the same as Janet's. Peter and Melissa were married at the Heinz Chapel on campus at the University of Pittsburgh on Saturday, February 25, 2006. My 92-year-old mom also attended the wedding with us and was thrilled to see her grandson get married in that famous chapel which she had toured many years earlier.

Julie and Laura were bridesmaids although Julie just became ill. She had a nasty wound on her back and thought it may have been a spider bite. Fortunately, she was well enough to participate as a bridesmaid, but on the return flight to Florida became feverish. We were all concerned.

On Monday morning, she went to an emergency room and when the doctor on call saw Julie's infection he was alarmed. What Julie thought was a spider bite was actually MRSA, a deadly flesh-eating disease. MRSA is a staph infection, Methicillin-Resistant Staphylococcus Aureus, and is unaffected by most antibiotics. Often, it quickly kills people. That doctor immediately checked Julie into the hospital where she had surgery the following day. The surgeon cut out the infected area, but could not close the wound since it had to heal from the inside out. Julie just had her own harrowing experience and survived.

36
PROSTATE PROBLEM

To celebrate Janet's birthday in June 2006, my 'three amigos' and I booked an 11-day Eastern Mediterranean Cruise, sailing from and ending in Rome. We arrived a couple of days early, rented an apartment, and spent two days sightseeing. We walked everywhere and this time toured the Roman Colosseum. As an architect, I found that 50,000-seat arena built 2000 years ago mind-boggling.

Of course, the cruise itself was fabulous and we enjoyed such interesting places as the Greek islands of Santorini (with its spectacular views), Rhodes (where we swam in the Aegean Sea), Mykanos (whose layout was purposely chaotic to confuse invading pirates), and then onto Istanbul (shopping at the Grand Bazaar, the world's largest), Ephesus (where the apostle John settled), Athens (fulfilling one of my heart's desires by visiting the Parthenon, which fascinated me since my days as an art history student at Columbia), and finally Pompeii (with its remarkable excavation) and Naples. On the ship we indulged ourselves with its renowned cuisine and a variety of dessert delicacies.

After returning home, I visited Dr. Ozer, my internist, for my yearly medical check-up along with blood work. He phoned me days later and said my PSA count—an indicator of prostate cancer—was elevated and recommended I have a biopsy.

My first thought was that any blood analysis after a cruise would likely be skewered because of ingesting its rich and lavish diet including a fresh omelet every morning; I ate nearly two dozen eggs in ten days. In years past when I had my annual check-up after a summer cruise my cholesterol spiked and Dr. Ozer routinely recommended I take a natural herb to lower my cholesterol. Normally, I follow doctor's orders, but in those cases ignored it and simply returned to my normal diet, which included few, if any eggs or desserts. Predictably, my cholesterol always dropped to an acceptable level.

Yet, this time I took his advice; I chose not to play Russian roulette with cancer.

One year earlier, in August 2005, I read on the sports pages the obituary of my dear friend, Gene Souder, the architect. He had just died of prostate cancer and was only 60 years old. I grieved for him and his family. He and his wife founded a soccer league in their community which established the sports interest. I hadn't seen Gene in years, but still considered him a friend as we worked together at The Lawrence Group and beyond, helping each other with drafting in the mid 1980s. He was a gifted architect and the only one from whom I solicited help to complete my projects. Actually, we helped each other when facing impending deadlines.

I had the biopsy done, but never gave it another thought. It took several weeks, and I became more confident with the passage of time that the results would be negative. Finally, the doctor performing the biopsy telephoned me and told me rather casually that *I had prostate cancer.*

Janet and I were stunned; that was *not* the result we expected. Three of the ten samples of the biopsy tested positive with a value of six on the Gleason scale, a measurement of the severity of the cancer. Seven was in the red (critical) range. Once again, it was hard to believe this was happening to me.

How did I get prostate cancer? I had a prostate infection in January 1985, of unknown origin, but merely months later as I was biting into my second glazed doughnut at a men's retreat, the Holy Spirit actually spoke to me and said, *"That's your problem!"* At that moment I realized sugar was my enemy.

Also in 1982, when I prayed about loving Julie more and the Holy Spirit spoke those two words, *"Fast desserts,"* was that also a warning that went unheeded?

Whether or not my self-analysis was accurate, I needed to act quickly before that prostate cancer metastasized. Cancer got my attention!

I phoned Dr. Ozer to ask him one question, "Who in the United States would be the best urologist for prostate cancer?" Immediately, he mentioned a Dr. Walsh from Johns Hopkins, but quickly added that he would likely be unavailable since he was on a speaking tour promoting his new technique for surgery. However, one of his protégé's practiced right here in West Palm Beach. That's how I connected with Dr. Neill Borland, the urologist.

Because of my age, 62, and good physical condition, Dr. Borland strongly recommended that I have a radical prostatectomy that Dr. Walsh had perfected. That procedure surgically removes the prostate, reduces bleeding, and would be the most certain way to eliminate cancer. There are other procedures treating prostate cancer, all with their own risk factors and success rates: injecting radioactive pellets in the prostate (Janet's brother, Willard, had that done which was successful), computerized surgery to remove the prostate, or simply monitoring the cancer regularly. It was decision time.

That night while cutting an apple into quarters, part of it was rotten and I simply cut out a rotten part while preserving the good. Immediately, I thought of my prostate and what Dr. Borland recommended. Cut out the 'cancer' to preserve the body.

Initially, I wanted nothing to do with any radical procedure, but this was a life or death situation—*my life or my death*. One's perspective changes when it becomes personal. As a result I asked myself what would be the best way to live another day. Naturally, Janet and I prayed about this decision, and we had peace about surgery. I phoned Dr. Borland the next day and told him surgery was affirmative.

Dr. Borland cautioned me that patients having a radical prostatectomy may bleed and suggested I have three units of my own blood available. Do I like needles? Of course not! However, I enjoy living more than I have a disdain for needles. I went to the nearest blood bank for the next three weeks, gave a unit of blood each time, and they were delivered to the hospital the day of surgery.

Surgery was performed Wednesday morning, September 27, 2006, at a hospital in West Palm Beach. Along with Janet, one of my Christian friends arrived at the hospital and prayed for me. Surgery lasted about three-and-a-half hours as Dr. Borland removed my prostate. He used one unit of my blood and was hopeful no cancer remained. Neither radiation nor chemotherapy were required.

However, glitches are everpresent. People in the medical field routinely ask a patient if he is allergic to anything. I had always been allergic to having any tape applied directly on my skin.

My worst experiences was at Camp Columbia, the pre-season football camp. For whatever ill-conceived reason, I taped one of my ankles for one of our practices. The next day my entire lower leg was grotesquely swollen with gigantic blisters and an entire layer of skin on my heel literally fell off. It was repulsive, but I showed it to our head football coach, Buff Donelli (who coached the Pittsburgh Steelers in the 1940s); he had never seen anything like it. I have super-sensitive skin.

After surgery I had a Foley catheter inserted and the tubing was *taped* to my right thigh. By the third day my thigh was inflamed. Although I told the staff I was allergic to tape, that bit of information apparently fell through the cracks. Knowing my sensitive skin, I simply told Dr. Borland to have the tape removed and within a week my thigh would be fine. A nurse removed the tape which caused some tearing of my skin, but within a week the skin irritation was healed.

Sadly, there was another problem. Some men react poorly to a Foley catheter as it causes spasms; I was one of them. While in the hospital I never felt any spasms because of pain medication. Before being released, however, all the meds were removed and that's when I felt the pain. Fortunately, they lasted only about ten to fifteen seconds each and I had about half dozen daily.

After two weeks of convalescing at home, I would return to Dr.Borland's office for my follow-up appointment. I was pleased to begin my own count-down before the catheter would be removed.

Finally, on day zero I went to my appointment and Dr. Borland removed the catheter, but to keep it off, I needed to urinate. Believe me, I have never been so motivated to urinate in my entire life. Fortunately, every-thing worked and I was pleased to be rid of that catheter. Better yet, *I was cancer-free*. This prostate cancer qualifies as '*my harrowing experience number six!*'

37
THE FALL

URING SPRING BREAK of 2007, Janet, Julie, Laura, and I booked an Eastern Caribbean Cruise which are such fun-loving vacations. The days are usually sun-drenched and most passengers, especially those from the north, simply love to sun-bathe at poolside listening to the sounds of a steel band while sipping the drink-of-the-day. We've seen so many lobster-red people who were simply naïve about the intensity of the tropical sun. Yet, I'm the one who had the accident.

I fell down a half-flight of stairs. It was embarrassing, but at least I never seriously injured myself as there was carpeting on the nosing of the treads instead of metal which would have torn up my flesh. I merely scraped my left shin with a seven-inch brush burn.

Guys in construction always get nicked so seeing blood was no cause for alarm; I washed my leg, but sought no medical attention.

Years earlier, I had an accident on one of my projects that even turned my stomach.

While trying to avoid stepping on the lid of an opened paint can, I lost my balance and backed into a metal storm panel lying on the floor. That storm panel sliced into the back of my right ankle and nearly severed my Achilles tendon. I put a band-aid on it, not one of my better moments.

The next day when I showed Janet my wound, she went bonkers. Because the wound was so deep, she thought she literally saw my tendon. Immediately, she took me to the emergency room where the attending physician said he couldn't stitch the wound because I had waited too long. He put on a real bandage on it and it healed, although there is a ragged scar to remind me of that little misadventure.

On the cruise ship that day I simply did not want to go to the ship's infirmary since it was merely a brush burn. While our ship was docked in the Bahamas, we went to a beach where I soaked my leg in the salty ocean water thinking that would be therapeutic.

Instead, it got worse. By the end of the cruise, my lower left leg was infected and swollen.

Upon returning home, Janet drove me to the emergency room once again to where the attending physician's assistant (PA) took a sample for a biopsy and wrote prescriptions for antibiotics. I took the antibiotics faithfully and was pleased to see my leg healing. Per her instructions I returned to the emergency room the following week to have the wound checked and find out the results of the biopsy. We saw the same physician's assistant and then she dropped the bomb.

That brush burn had become infected with MRSA!

Without knowing what type of infection was affecting my shin, that thoughtful PA prescribed antibiotics for MRSA. By taking such a conservative approach, she may very well have saved my life or at least my leg.

We heard a story of a person similar to mine. While on a cruise ship a man got cut, it became MRSA, and two days later he died. That could have been me. This seemingly innocuous mishap evolved into *'my harrowing experience number seven!*

38
STENOSIS

AFTER HAVING A radical prostatectomy to surgically remove my malignancy, I had two PSA tests done yearly…one by Dr. Ozer and the other by Dr. Borland. My PSA remains negligible, and I am free of cancer.

After Dr. Borland examined me in December 2007, he casually asked how I was doing. I decided to tell him. Five years earlier I tried to jump a small puddle of water and nearly couldn't because the Stenosis had atrophied my calf muscles. Those muscles were necessary to run and jump, but were slowly dying. He suggested I see an orthopedic doctor since medical breakthroughs may have been discovered for Stenosis.

I took his advice and made an appointment with an orthopedic doctor on our insurance plan in January 2008. Before seeing the orthopod, however, one of his associates performed an electro-myography test that recorded the electrical activity pulsating through the nerves in my legs.

When the test was completed, that doctor informed me that in a teenager the electrical impulses in the legs travel at 60 milliamps/second while in an 80-year-old they travel at 40 milliamps/second. My readings were in the high 30s. Were my legs really worse than an 80-year-old? Apparently, they were. Furthermore, he said I likely had Charko-Marie Tooth syndrome, a condition in which the calf muscles atrophy while the rest of the body remains muscular.

Now I was ready to see the orthopedic doctor; what would he do? He ordered an MRI on my lower back…it was done. He prescribed physical therapy for my legs…I did it. Then, he ran out of options as there were no medical breakthroughs for Stenosis. I would simply have to live with my sore back and atrophied calf muscles.

As people age many have a tendency to gain weight as their metabolism slows down. I had ballooned up to 230 pounds and my mid-section expanded accordingly. Janet, conversely, had been going to the gym for years and worked hard to maintain her trim figure besides monitoring her diet. I never envisioned my dear wife becoming a gym rat while I became a couch potato, but the evidence was apparent…check our waistlines.

Janet, however, had a solution for me…lose weight. She thought that by losing weight, I would relieve the stress in my lower back. I love Janet, but considered her diagnosis as naïve. A person born with a congenital condition—spinal Stenosis—would not miraculously correct that by simply losing weight. I had seen two different orthopedic doctors and neither offered relief or even hope.

Janet persisted; actually, she began to nag. She reminded me that Dr. John Whelton, her rheumatologist, insisted that she lose weight and her knees would feel better and he was right. She had visited her own orthopedic surgeon who told her that because of the stress in her knees, she would require knee joint replacement surgery some day. When she lost 40 pounds, however, the weight loss eased the stress in her knees and she not only looked better, but no longer needed surgery. Losing weight benefited Janet.

Janet's nagging finally wore me down. I made an appointment to see Dr. John Whelton in December 2008, for one reason and one reason only. I expected Dr. Whelton to tell Janet that *losing weight would not help my back*. As well as she knew me, she did not experience my discomfort. Not only did I have Stenosis with arthritis exasperating that condition, but I fell off a scaffold nine years earlier nearly crushing my spine; that was a triple whammy damaging my back.

Prior to my appointment in December with Dr. Whelton, I picked up a copy of the MRI from the orthopedic doctor's office taken earlier that year. As I checked into the appointment, I turned over to the receptionist the MRI for the good doctor's review prior to seeing me.

After I got settled in the exam room and waited a few minutes, Dr. Whelton entered and immediately said, *"You need surgery!"* Incredulously, I looked at him like that proverbial deer staring into headlights. I was speechless. Why didn't he just tell Janet that losing weight would not help my back?

As a rheumatologist his approach to good health is to try any and all natural means to heal a person other than surgery; which I knew he considered a last resort. However, in viewing the MRI, he realized my condition was so severe it could only be corrected with surgery. He even showed me the MRI and said that as an architect, I would understand the stress patterns shown. I didn't fully comprehend that MRI, but there appeared to be an explosion in the middle of my back and I knew that couldn't be good. As an afterthought he did tell Janet and me that losing weight would not improve my back.

Dr. Whelton insisted that surgery would be merely for technical reasons;

could it be that simple? With the Stenosis and ever-increasing arthritis the openings behind my spinal column enclosing the nerves to my legs were progressively diminishing. As a result those nerves were constantly constricted reducing the electrical impulses stimulating my legs and my calf muscles were slowly eroding. Surgery would enlarge those openings, eliminate the constriction of the nerves and allow greater electrical impulses to stimulate the muscles in my legs. He offered me hope; with greater electrical stimulation, perhaps my calf muscles could regenerate.

I found it disconcerting that in reviewing the exact same MRI, the latest orthopedic doctor did nothing while Dr. Whelton insisted I needed surgery. How can the diagnosis by two doctors be so radically different? I've pondered that question and concluded that an orthopedic surgeon was not trained to correct Stenosis in the back; it was beyond his area of expertise. A neurosurgeon skilled in correcting spinal disorders was needed, and John Whelton knew the man.

He made an appointment for me on April 8, 2009, with Dr. Barth Green, a neurosurgeon in Miami who specialized in the spinal chord disorders. Dr. Green is Professor and Chairman of Neurological Surgery at "The U"— the University Of Miami Miller School Of Medicine. Another challenge in my life was unfolding.

Janet is active and gets things done. While driving in early 2009, she phoned her school board insurance to inquire whether or not Dr. Green and the Jackson Memorial Hospital, where surgery would be performed, were covered by her insurance. Both were and my back surgery would be approved.

Several people asked me how in the world did I ever get Dr. Barth Green as my surgeon. He's a superstar among spinal surgeons and is highly selective. The truth is always the best explanation. *Only* because Janet so lovingly nagged me to lose weight did I make that appointment with Dr. Whelton, fully expecting him to tell Janet that losing weight would not help my back. He did that, but also recommended surgery and referred me to Dr. Barth Green. Quite literally, *I only responded to Janet's nagging!*

39
PREPARING FOR BACK SURGERY

I LEARNED SOMETHING ABOUT "elective" back surgery. I literally had to be in perfect health before Dr. Green would even lay a finger on me. Never before have I ever been so carefully scrutinized prior to surgery. Of course, my brain tumor and prostate cancer surgeries were life and death situations and hardly optional. While the back surgery may not appear life threatening, my real choice was whether or not I chose to become paralyzed. It was only a matter of time before those calf muscles would die altogether and I'd be confined to a wheelchair for my remaining days. Seriously, I really had no choice.

Before my appointment with Dr. Green, on March 24, 2009, I drove to the Sylvester Cancer Center in Deerfield Beach, about forty five miles from Tequesta, to have another MRI of my back. This medical facility was part of the University of Miami Health System, and Dr. Green could access my MRI and see for himself the condition of my back.

On April 8, 2009, Janet and I drove to the University of Miami Health System Clinic in Miami to meet Dr. Green. We waited for nearly five hours before actually seeing him, but when facing such delicate surgery, why complain about waiting a few hours more?

While waiting, one of the nurse practitioners interviewed me to get relevant data for Dr. Green. One of her questions was whether or not I had ever passed out. I pondered momentarily before answering, "Yes!" I related to her the incident with the Xerox machine compressing my carotid artery, cutting off blood to my brain and passing out. She said that didn't count, although it became my near-death experience number one.

Finally, Dr. Green arrived and greeted me by saying "...*And you're still walking!*" He had already assessed the severity of my back, but instead of dwelling on the obvious, we talked about cruising, one of our favorite subjects. Dr. Green is likely the most personable doctor I've ever met. He was also keenly observant and noticed I had a skin rash on my fingers and wanted that cleared up before surgery. Other than Stenosis, I had to be in perfect health as he wanted no complications.

His diagnosis was "Lumbar Stenosis" and "Thoracic-Lumbar Spondylosis" (whatever that is). In a letter to Dr. John Whelton describing our consultation of April 8ᵗʰ, Dr. Green made the observation: *"I do not think I have ever seen a more severe case of Stenosis."* Now Dr. Green is a seasoned neurosurgeon and is not prone to hyperbole. For him to write those words indicated my back was far worse than even I suspected. Yet, I still functioned normally…somehow the Lord sustained me. He continued, *"The risks of death, paralysis, numbness, hemorrhage, spinal fluid leak, impotence, incontinence, failure to fuse, infection, past history of MRSA, need for further surgery, etc. He fully understood and signed the informed consent."* What had I gotten into?

Initially, we scheduled surgery for June 23, 2009, after Dr. Green's vacation, but Janet realized that it would benefit me to have surgery earlier and we rescheduled it for Thursday, May 21ˢᵗ, before his vacation. The next six weeks became action-packed.

The next day, April 9ᵗʰ, I faxed to Dr. Ozer the script requested by Dr. Green prior to surgery. Foremost, Dr. Green wanted medical clearance that I could tolerate surgery, meaning he wanted my medical history along with a current physical with "full systems review." I also needed blood work, an EKG (since I was older than 55), chest X-rays (PA and Lateral), and a chemical stress test. My appointment with Dr. Ozer was made for Tuesday, May 12ᵗʰ. I would have preferred it earlier since surgery was scheduled only nine days later. There wasn't much wiggle room should anything go wrong.

On Monday, April 13ᵗʰ I made an appointment with a dermatologist to clear up my skin rash, and he helped me. I theorized that I had some type of parasite from working in my back yard with my bare hands, but he said I was allergic to something in my own environment. He prescribed a hand cream for me.

A couple days later I went to Around and About Orthotics, Inc., a medical facility that makes braces or casts for various parts of the body. I needed a body brace from shoulders to waist, front and rear to stabilize my back after surgery. While wearing only a T-shirt on my upper body, the technicians wrapped me with a gauze-like material and then doused me with water. That gauze-like material hardened instantly and became like a plaster cast around my torso, not the most comfortable feeling. That cast became the mold from which they made the plastic shell that, once in place, would stabilize my back for the sixteen weeks after surgery. I felt like the bionic man.

On Thursday, April 23rd, at Dr. Green's request, I drove to Deerfield Beach, Florida once again, to have an additional CT scan taken of my brain. Although I had brain surgery nearly thirty years earlier, Dr. Green wanted to check it out for himself. I had annual CAT scans for five years following brain surgery and those scans showed no evidence of any further tumor activity. That CT scan confirmed my brain was healthy.

Four days later on Monday, April 27th, I traveled to Deerfield Beach to have yet another MRI of my back. Apparently, the MRI and CT scan could not be performed on the same day, something about too much radiation which was the reason they were scheduled four days apart. It made me wonder, however, how much radiation was actually bombarding my body.

On April 30th, I picked up my back brace from Around and About, Inc. It was like a turtle shell from neck to waist with separate front and back custom molded plastic shells held together with three Velcro straps on each side. When I was fourteen years old, I remember how excited it was to put on a football uniform for the first time with the shoulder pads, hip pads, and pants with knee and thigh pads, jersey top and helmet. The thought of wearing that back brace for four months did not thrill me.

On May 5, 2009, I saw the dermatologist and we were both pleased because my skin rash was healed. Dr. Green would also be pleased.

There was a bump in the road, however.

On Tuesday, May 12th, only nine days before surgery, I went to my appointment with Dr. Ozer. Only moments before actually seeing Dr. Ozer, his office manager told me he could not administer the chemical stress test, a cardiologist was needed. On hearing those words, I nearly exploded! *Why didn't you tell me a month earlier?* My concern about no wiggle room suddenly became reality.

I didn't even have a cardiologist and arranging a chemical stress test within days would be nearly impossible. But wait, I knew Dr. Vargas, a cardiologist, who had been treating my mom for the last 11 years. Immediately, I telephoned Dr. Vargas' office, explained my predicament and he graciously accommodated me by scheduling the chemical stress test for Monday, May 18th. Maintaining good relationships are vital.

Aside from the chemical stress test fiasco, my appointment with Dr. Ozer proceeded well. Since we had a 26-year history he knew I was in excellent health, but commented that I was about to undergo the most demanding activity any person would ever endure—major surgery. Of course, I already had a craniotomy and radical prostatectomy and healed well afterwards. The back surgery, however, would present a different challenge as I was about to discover.

I had an EKG in Dr. Ozer's office, walked to an adjacent building for my chest X-rays and finally went to a nearby lab for blood work. At the lab I ran into an architect friend and we reminisced about how we had our own ten-event "Olympic Games" thirty five years earlier. He didn't know it, but he would crush me now since I couldn't even run. Life is so unpredictable; it's good to have some fun along the way.

That Friday, May 15th, I had a consultation with Dr. Vargas regarding the chemical stress test and that day he, officially, became my cardiologist.

I went to Dr. Vargas' office for the chemical stress test that Monday. How stressful could it be since I'd be lying down. There were three people monitoring this test: a doctor (in case I had an adverse reaction to the chemicals being pumped into me), the person administering the test and a nurse. Although it lasted only five minutes, those three encouraged me by counting down the minutes and finally the seconds before it was over. Having those chemicals rev up my heart was not the most pleasant experience, but at least it was over quickly.

There were so many medical details to complete and things bogged down. My instructions were to have all the information from Dr. Ozer to Dr. Green's office 72 hours prior to surgery. I sent a Fax Memorandum to Dr. Ozer's office reminding him of the schedule. Finally, his office manager assured me that everything had been sent on Monday, May 18th. The result from the chemical stress test had yet to be evaluated and that analysis would be sent the day before surgery. It would have annoyed me enormously for surgery to be postponed because somebody failed to pass on vital information. It became tense, but Dr. Green's office finally received all the required data.

Tuesday, May 19th, was my pre-op visit. Once again, I drove to Miami, had back and chest X-rays and gave a unit of my blood for surgery. Finally, everything was complete for the main event.

40
THE DAY-BEFORE
SQUIRREL CAGE

IT WOULD HAVE been pleasant to relax the day before surgery, but it became the exact opposite. I was frantic with activity. As a contractor I had just completed a project, a bedroom/bathroom addition for a handicapped child in a local community. It wasn't large, but the unexpected happens.

I planned to go to the building department, obtain the "Certificate of Completion," make a copy for the owner, pick up my final check and deposit it in the bank before 2:00 PM. I knew after surgery I would be out of commission indefinitely and that Wednesday, May 20th, would be my final day working for some time.

The surprise came suddenly!

At the building department a secretary informed me it had not received the "pull-off" test for the Spanish "S" concrete tile from the roofing contractor and would not issue the Certificate of Completion without it. Immediately, I saw my optimistic plan hit the wall. I left the building department dejected and immediately phoned the roofing contractor. Sure enough, he confirmed the pull-off test had not been done although all roofing, including inspections, had been completed.

An hour later I returned to the building department to determine what needed to be done to get the certificate when a miracle occurred. The same secretary who told me earlier about the "pull-off" test sought me out and gave me the "Certificate of Completion." I was speechless, then thanked her profusely, but never mentioned the pull-off test. With certificate in hand I dashed out, back on schedule.

Immediately, I made a copy, delivered it to the owner, picked up my final check and rushed to my nearest bank to deposit it before 2:00 PM, with merely minutes to spare. My plan worked, but not without a hefty dose of anxiety.

Then, another one of my architectural clients unexpectedly phoned me that afternoon and said he needed the final drawings for his home renovation. He hadn't phoned in weeks and if he waited just one day longer, I would have been unable to help him. Fortunately, I had completed his work. After returning to my home office, I gathered his drawings, went to my printer, had a number of sets printed, drove to his home where I signed and sealed those prints for permitting.

It was now nearly 6:00 PM, but there was still work to be done.

Whenever I go on vacation, the day before is usually hectic since I'm writing checks and preparing "to do" lists for others. My surgery was similar as I wrote business checks to subcontractors. If I didn't write those checks that evening, there was no telling when they would be paid and subs aren't known for their patience. That was the reason I needed to deposit the check before 2:00 PM; the money would be available the next business day.

Janet was not pleased with me. We made a motel reservation near the Jackson Memorial Hospital and expected to relax the evening before surgery. That never happened. We didn't leave for Miami until after 10:00 PM and after driving nearly 90 miles didn't check into the motel until nearly midnight. We were both exhausted. Surgery was imminent.

41
BACK SURGERY

I WAS NUMBER TWO on Dr. Green's card that Thursday, but was instructed to be in the waiting room by 9:30 AM. Don't ask me why, but Janet and I followed orders and then waited for hours. The first surgery took longer than expected and the time was now late afternoon. I became apprehensive thinking my surgery may be postponed and did not want to repeat that fire drill one more time, perhaps a month later.

Of course, as we waited, there was a diversion. By late morning a hospital administrator approached Janet and me and had me complete a living will on the spot. Why would she do that? Clearly, there were risks involved with this merely technical surgery that Dr. Whelton recommended. Death, apparently, was one of them.

Finally, around 4:30 PM a nurse escorted me to the prep room as my surgery was imminent. I greeted Dr. Green in his hospital scrubs before he made a 12-inch mark on my back for the incision. I kissed Janet goodbye, was given anesthesia, and quickly conked out.

Many hours later, around 3:30 AM., I woke up in the recovery room. Still groggy from the anesthesia, I simply thanked God that I was still alive and my back surgery was now history.

Surgery was completed about 1:30 AM and involved cutting off the bones enclosing the spinal cord behind vertebrae T11, T12, L1, L2, L3, L4, L5 and S1. The arthritis on those bones was scraped off before the surgical team ground up those bones, added a paste to the bone powder and replaced the new pliable bone material at their respective vertebrae with larger openings to enclose the spinal cord. Obviously, Dr. Green and his team were careful not to damage my spinal cord while those bones were being cut from each vertebrae and then securing that new pliable bone material in place. Sounds incredibly delicate, doesn't it? Thank you, Dr. Green and your surgical team.

After surgery Dr. Green sought out Janet and Julie, who joined her mom for support and comfort and told them surgery was successful, I did well and was in the recovery room. They were both relieved and grateful. He continued by saying how sore his hands were by working on my bones.

Although that was the best news for Janet to hear, she became apprehensive about walking to the motel in the middle of the night in, admittedly, not Miami's finest neighborhood. Dr. Green, once again, became their knight in shining armor as he personally drove Janet and Julie to their motel, several blocks away. I've never heard of any surgeon ever doing that, particularly after a grueling 18-hour day of surgery.

After spending several hours in the recovery room, which was becoming only too familiar, I was taken to my own room. Of my major surgeries, the back surgery was the most traumatic. Aside from my chest being numb for days, I literally had tubes coming out of my body in numerous places, one of which was a drain from my back that was hooked up to something called a hemovac.

Imagine for a moment *how* back surgery is performed. I was lying face down on a flat metal table for nearly eight hours and the surgical team hooked me up to a machine that mechanically breathed for me. Being unconscious, I couldn't raise my chest to breath for myself. It's no wonder my chest was numb for days after surgery.

When surgery is done on a person's back, initially every movement is usually slow and painful. Yet, the very next day my nurse had me walk down the hall using a walker for support. She even showed me how to walk up stairs, sideways if necessary, and I gamely walked up a half flight of stairs. The nurses were pleased by my efforts.

After several days Dr. Green came into my room and gave me some rather chilling news. We all knew about the Stenosis with arthritis, but at the T11 and T12 joint there was *a tumor pressing against the nerves that were so constricted they were virtually screaming to be released!* Dr. Green removed the tumor and released the pressure. None of my doctors (the orthopedic doctor, Dr. Whelton or Dr. Green) ever mentioned the presence of a tumor, but when my back was opened, there it was…*surprise!!*

I theorized that falling off the scaffold ten years earlier and severely jolting my back and cracking two vertebrae likely caused the tumor which was slowly paralyzing me. I believe Dr. Green chose to wait until the biopsy was completed before giving me the good news that the tumor was benign. When I viewed my own MRI at Dr. Whelton's office five months earlier, what I perceived as an "explosion" in my back was likely that tumor.

One of doctors on the surgical team asked me about the neurosurgeon for brain surgery thirty years earlier. (My back surgery was just 25 days shy of the 30th anniversary of brain surgery; what a day to remember). I told him Dr. McFarland was my surgeon and although they never met, he knew him by reputation.

My two neurosurgeons just happened to be among the world's finest and the reality is that I sought out neither of them. I just happened to be under the care of physicians who referred them to me. Once again, the Lord directed my steps.

On Wednesday, May 28th, I was released from Jackson Memorial Hospital and my wonderful wife drove to Miami to bring me home. I needed constant care and could not be left alone. Normally, Janet would care for me as she had throughout this ordeal, but still had one more week of teaching and all her sick/personal days were gone. If she missed any more work, her pay would be docked and we couldn't afford that. Julie and Laura likewise could not take time off from their jobs.

Sadly, Janet and I had not formed any close relationships with anybody in the church we were attending, not that we didn't try. I had been active in men's meetings for the past year and actually spoke to about 35 men about my upcoming surgery at a prayer breakfast on Friday, May 15th. The men prayed for me and for that I was grateful, but not one person from the church phoned either me or my family after surgery. We were disappointed.

Laura, however, came to the rescue. She went to a different church and arranged for her friends, who were also praying for me, to care for me during Janet's final week of teaching.

For my convalescence Janet arranged to get a hospital bed which we set up in our great room. I wore my back brace faithfully whenever out of bed and used a "bone-growth stimulator" around my lower back for four hours each day for 16 weeks. While not so obvious, I still considered my back surgery as another dance with death, *"my harrowing experience number eight!"*

42
FACEBOOK

URING THAT SUMMER of 2009 while convalescing, Julie signed me up for Facebook. Naïvely, I asked her, "What's Facebook?" When we moved to South Florida in 1972, I lost contact with nearly all my college friends. I kept in touch, albeit infrequently, with Victor, my fellow Fiji (Phi Gamma Delta) in California and contacted Tom Chorba, one of my football teammates, in New Jersey, regarding our 40th college reunion, but that was all. Then, Facebook kicked in.

Bob Klingensmith, another teammate living in California, found me through Facebook and invited Janet and me to attend a mini-reunion at the Columbia-Dartmouth football game in Hanover, New Hampshire that October. While Janet has zero interest in sports, she delights in autumn, with its changing leaves and nippy temperatures, all creating an atmosphere conducive for meeting friendly people. When I asked her about going, she jumped on it.

Soon I connected with other teammates: Steve Franke, Roger Dennis, Dean Mottard (a helicopter pilot in Viet Nam with six hundred missions and shot down three times), Barry Nazarian and several fraternity brothers. *All of a sudden, I had friends—thank you, Facebook!*

With nostalgia soaring, I wrote a brief personal history since graduating Columbia—my "Dear Friends" letter—and e-mailed to several of my long-lost teammates and fraternity brothers. Most people would not have the time or inclination to write a personal history, but, while convalescing, I had an ample supply of time, and nostalgia provided the motivation.

With their summer vacations winding down in late July, Janet and Laura simply couldn't resist the appeal of another Caribbean cruise. Janet especially thought I could use a pleasant change after lying in a hospital bed for months; I just love her for that! So Janet and I (wearing back brace and bone growth stimulator), along with Julie and Laura, sailed away to the Western Caribbean. While in port, my three favorite ladies went ashore as I chilled out onboard, read a couple of books, and savored the fabulous cuisine. What a beautiful way to end summer vacation.

Wednesday, September 9th was the day of my 16-week appointment with Dr. Green. If he determined my new bones were growing properly, I would no longer need to wear the back brace or use the bone growth stimulator. I hoped for the best.

My faithful wife and best caregiver drove me to the appointment where the staff took a couple X-rays of my back before meeting Dr. Green. He was pleased with my progress and said with some humor— "no more back brace…burn it!" Also, I no longer needed the bone-growth stimulator or hospital bed. I was given an elastic back brace to wear for the next couple months before beginning physical therapy in December.

Healing from back surgery took much longer than healing from brain surgery thirty years earlier. Fortunately, no hurricanes mauled South Florida that summer; I could not have installed any hurricane protection while convalescing.

After that vital appointment, I directed my attention to the mini-reunion in October and realized how much I had changed since Janet and I became born again Christians. How would my former teammates respond to us?

For weeks before the reunion, as I was doing rehab for my back in our swimming pool, I prayed fervently for the people planning to attend. Not knowing if any of my teammates were believers or not, Janet and I needed to be those *ambassadors for Christ* (2 Corinthians 5:20) and let our '*light*' shine (Matthew 5:16).

On Thursday, October 22nd, we took our flight from West Palm Beach to Manchester, New Hampshire, and drove our rental car to our motel in Nashua. We arrived late at night exhausted and collapsed in bed. The following morning Janet and I met for breakfast with Steve and Diane Franke, Bob and Nancy Klingensmith, and Dean Mottard, and quickly renewed friendships after more than four decades.

After breakfast, Bob—who took me under his wing—and Nancy drove Janet and me through the New Hampshire countryside to simply enjoy the scenery and parked at a quaint New England town named Keene. There, we walked around the town green and took photos of their vintage gazebo while kicking fall leaves; we loved the cooler temperature. We miss autumn in South Florida after enduring an extended summer with its heat.

That afternoon, Janet and I took a helicopter ride for an aerial tour of the colorful foliage. Dean arranged for that activity and really wanted to fly one himself, but his friends from the helicopter business kept him grounded. The leaves were colorful, although the tour people told us they peaked a week and a half earlier, but they still looked like a beautiful patch-work quilt to us. We also had our first bird's-eye view of a pumpkin patch which we never see in South Florida.

That night our group had dinner at Georgio's and I wore my Columbia letterman blazer for the first time in over forty years. Janet chatted with many of my teammates and she was a hit. Bob, a wine connoisseur, brought his own magnum from California for everybody's pleasure, and Tom Chorba challenged us with a spelling contest won by Steve Franke. I was impressed that many of my teammates had remained married for more than 40 years.

Bob, the prime mover, told us the bus to Hanover would be leaving by mid-morning on game day. Rain was in the forecast. Regardless of the weather, everybody was excited just being together and the bus ride became a party on wheels. Steve arranged for game tickets and Columbia hats for our group and, because of the rain forecast, Dean had a tent installed outside the stadium for shelter as we enjoyed our box lunches.

While huddling under the tent, our lunch time was about to become supercharged with unexpected guests. Students from the Columbia's marching band were walking across the street, but because it was drizzling, Rich Forzani invited them to take shelter under our tent. Although reluctant at first, the band members finally joined us. Columbia had what is called a "scramble band" that would never compete seriously with a highly organized band performing crisp maneuvers; nevertheless, it was undeniably unique.

Of course, there was wine and everybody imbibed. Despite the rain, there was a setting for an incredible spontaneous tailgate party. Bob suggested we sing a familiar Columbia fight song and with a little urging from teammates, the band began playing. It was electrifying and everybody sang with gusto.

People of every generation think they have a secret known only to them. The graduates of '66C, who were now in our mid sixties, had their secret. Bob and several others started singing a rather off-color version of that familiar fight song and were stunned when the band members, all in their late teens or early twenties, not only sang along with Bob, but embellished it with lyrics of their own. The sixties crowd roared, they knew our secret. There was an instant bonding between generations. They were just like us, only 45 years younger. Janet couldn't understand how we arranged to have the marching band entertain us, but I told her that really was a "chance" encounter.

The game itself was anticlimactic—sorry Coach. There was steady rain and I simply couldn't understand how the drum majorette for Dartmouth could perform in such a skimpy outfit while I was bundled up like an Eskimo heading for the Arctic tundra while toting an umbrella. We sat through the first half, but Janet and I boarded the bus to sit out the second half and we were not alone. There were plenty of snacks along with the ubiquitous bottles of wine. The return bus trip passed quickly.

That evening our group planned to have dinner at another local restaurant, only it couldn't accommodate all of us and spontaneity kicked in. Quickly, we decided to have a pizza party at the breakfast room in our motel—*doesn't everybody love pizza?*

Roger Dennis and I reminisced about passing our swimming tests at Columbia merely weeks before graduation; Pete Salzer's wife, Linda, a teacher herself, immediately bonded with Janet; Bill Corcorran reminded me of a botched tackle-eligible play designed for him except I was in the game when that play was called and missed the pass from Archie Roberts. Barry Nazarian entertained everybody by simply being himself.

Janet and I had a fabulous time which far exceeded all expectations. Did our 'lights' shine? One of the guys wrote this e-mail to me days later: "…Speaking of preaching, to me you and Janet represent all that I consider good in people that truly believe. You are warm, welcoming, caring, sincere, and NOT judgmental. Looking back I am embarrassed that you two spent so much time listening to my experiences and I spent absolutely none listening to yours. At any rate, I believe that you guys give Christians a very good name, and that is one of the highest compliments I could give you. Yeah, I know, I may well 'burn,' but with friends like you praying for me there just might be a little hope at the end of this wonderful winding trail." Apparently, Janet and I were witnesses.

Barry, our team's 'poet laureate,' was asked to summarize the events of the weekend and particularly our interaction with the Columbia band; following were his final words:

> "We can rail against the fading of the light. We can even bench in
> the 300's or race a hundred miles as some of us have done. But if it
> is not yet late in that final quarter, there is no longer any denying

that we have entered into it, and the digits on the clock flashing through the haze at the distant end of that field keep ticking down.

Because the Sixties Generation is now literally the sixties generation, and although we have for decades accepted the fact that we are no longer on campus, we are now old enough to be aware emotionally as well as intellectually that in time we won't be here at all.

And in confronting that one final paradox even greater than the confrontation which allowed us to face different people who were yet ourselves, it seemed to me that the real wavering truth humming through that entire chance meeting, that feeling of comfort along with uneasiness, the happy endorsement of those we faced undercut by some suppressed longing, the indignation of our disbelief over who we no longer were tempered by our acceptance of who we had become, was merely the realization that after we are gone the band will play on, boys.

The band *will* play on."

Clearly, Barry was very much aware of our own mortality, yet, life as we know it will continue. Since all of us will complete our days and return to the earth ('dust to dust, ashes to ashes'), I've prayed daily for every one my mini-reunion friends and want them to be where I'll be going. I have an affection for my teammates that surprises even me.

I was also pleased to learn that Steve and Diane Franke lived in Houston. Two weeks later I had planned a business trip there to attend a barbeque to support a builder friend and promote his technique of erecting highly efficient 'green' structures. My flight would take me to the airport closest to Steve's home and when I phoned him about spending the first night in Houston with him, he promptly agreed.

Steve picked me up at the airport, drove me to his beautiful home where he and Diane were perfect hosts that evening. Reminiscing was so pleasant; Steve and I were the starting defensive tackles our junior year. The night before playing Dartmouth a mere 45 years earlier, he remembered the outstanding New England clam chowder we savored, one of my favorite memories as well. They also reminded me that I attended their wedding in Brooklyn in 1965, and even had pictures of my being there.

Another couple from the reunion, Pete and Linda Salzer, invited Janet and me to spend a weekend at their home in the Hamptons on Long

Island during Janet's upcoming Christmas break. She was excited about that invite and we went.

It was Friday, December 18, 2009, when we took our flight to LaGuardia Airport and began the drive in our rental car to the eastern tip of Long Island late at night. For the first time in my life I understood why it was named LONG Island—it was really long! While driving we heard on the radio disturbing reports about a blizzard heading toward the Northeast, expecting to dump 20 inches of snow exactly where we would be staying. Immediately, Janet realized our weekend would be curtailed as the following week we were planning to spend Christmas with Peter and Melissa in Fort Worth, Texas. We couldn't get stranded.

Finding Pete's home that night became high drama.

It was close to 11:00 PM, pitch black and I drove on unfamiliar roads and even with directions was nearly lost. I phoned Pete and he became my air-traffic controller guiding me every step of the way for the last five miles. Finally, we met in the middle of town, got out of our cars and embraced each other like a long-lost brothers. That was priceless.

We followed Pete to his home and although the hour was late, Janet and I enjoyed Pete and Linda for the next hour before retiring. We agreed with some sadness that our weekend would be shortened because of the impeding blizzard.

On Saturday morning, Pete and Linda took us for breakfast and we toured some of the local sites, but snow flurries were just beginning and it was time to leave. Pete graciously loaned me one his winter coats and gloves since I was ill-prepared for the frigid North.

Thank you, Pete. Janet insisted that I make a reservation at the same motel on Saturday night that we had booked for Sunday. To our surprise the motel was adjacent to our rental car drop-off. While unplanned by me, that was perfect and we know Who does things perfectly!

After checking into the motel, we hunkered down to wait out the blizzard. New York City got about 10 inches of snow that night, but the next day Janet and I bravely ventured into Manhattan as sightseers.

We were so impressed with the New Yorkers who helped our bus gain traction after it became stuck in snow. After our short bus ride we took a subway to Manhattan where we walked through Macy's, went to the Empire State Building (it was crowded and took us over two hours to get to the observation deck where it was really COLD), tried to find Mama's

Leone's unsuccessfully, but did find the Rockefeller Center's skating rink and enjoyed seeing the famous decorated Christmas Tree.

We made our lemonade that day (when you have a lemon, you make...). Fortunately, on Monday morning the flights from LaGuardia Airport were on schedule and we returned safely home to warm and sunny South Florida.

Later that week Janet, Julie, Laura, and I boarded our flight to Dallas/Ft. Worth airport where our son, Peter, met us. We celebrated Christmas with Peter and Melissa in their new home, three dogs and, of all things, snow. It was ironic that Janet and I experienced snowfall on consecutive weekends; it doesn't snow in South Florida.

For Peter's birthday, December 26th, we celebrated by seeing the movie *Avatar* while Laura shopped. Peter and Melissa were wonderful hosts and showed us many sites in the area. We were blessed celebrating Christmas together as a family, a first in many years.

43
THE SHOCKER

THE DISCOMFORT BEGAN on Monday, February 22, 2010. It wasn't pain, but rather an odd sensation on the left side of my chest, but when it persisted for the next two days, I became concerned. I purposely didn't tell Janet because she would have whisked me to the emergency room without blinking. Instead, I surreptitiously made an appointment with Dr. Vargas, my cardiologist, for Friday, the 26th. That odd sensation was near my heart.

At that time Janet and I had just began to visit another church, although we had known Pastor Norman and Judy Benz for nearly thirty years. It was January, 1981, when Norman was introduced to the congregation at Maranatha as a newcomer to the pastoral staff and we were part of the congregation. Our oldest daughter, Julie, and their oldest son, Jonathon, were the same age and attended the same high school and college at the same time. Pastor Norman baptized Janet and me as adults at Maranatha and I was the architect for interior improvements for his own church in the mid 1990's.

On Thursday, February 25th, we invited Norman and Judy to our home for dinner to rekindle our friendship.

The next day during my appointment with Dr. Vargas, I described to him what I was experiencing. If I took a deep breath or lay on my left side, there was discomfort in my chest. He assured me that it didn't sound like a heart problem because if I had angina, I could not induce the discomfort as described, but would be constant pain. I was relieved although he scheduled me for an EEG at his office on Monday.

After seeing Dr. Vargas, at his request I stopped at the Jupiter Medical Center (JMC) for a chest X-ray and blood work.

That weekend I finally told Janet what I had done and, once again, she was not pleased. My reason for seeing Dr. Vargas was that if something were wrong, we could control the situation better instead of being swept along with emergency room doctors in crisis mode.

Early Monday morning, Dr. Vargas unexpectedly phoned me and was somber. *My chest X-ray came back abnormal!* In medical parlance that is never good; what was happening now? Later that day, I had the EEG which was normal, but he scheduled me for a CT scan on my chest on Thursday, March 4th. I cannot count the number of scans I've had between the brain surgery, Stenosis, back surgery and now, my chest.

If I thought Dr. Vargas was somber on Monday, he was undeniably morose on Friday when I saw him to review the CT scan. It revealed a large mass in my left lung and he thought it may be malignant. He continued by saying the location of the mass was exceedingly perilous since it was so close to my heart with its major arteries. I sensed that he spoke to me as though I was a walking dead man.

Although another crisis was unfolding in my life, I failed to appreciate the gravity of his words; perhaps I was in denial and simply never thought of having cancer or dying. Remarkably, I had no fear.

Dr. Vargas arranged for me to have a PET scan on Monday, March 8th. The PET scan goes from the top of the head to the bottom of the feet to detect the evidence of cancer.

That weekend Janet and I went to a green market in West Palm Beach when Richard, Janet's brother, phoned me. He has doctorates in pharmacology and dentistry and was interested in medical issues; we discussed what was happening in my lung and surmised that if it were a tumor, it may be benign like the tumors in my brain and back.

That Monday I drove to a medical facility to have my first PET scan. The nurse injected me with a solution and I had to lie still for an hour and twenty minutes for it to fully circulate my vascular system. While lying there peacefully lost in my own thoughts, another patient spoke up and told me he had been smoking for forty years and it finally caught up to him. He had a touch of lung cancer, but assured me that with the current medications, lung cancer could be managed. While he was trying to comfort me, I was annoyed because he interrupted my peace and did not want to discuss cancer at all.

Finally, I had the PET scan which was similar to all others…the CAT, CT and MRI.

Early Tuesday, March 9th, Dr. Vargas phoned me with the results of the scan. He was upbeat while informing me there was no cancer elsewhere in my body other than what was happening in my chest. In effect he just told me that while I may have cancer, it had not yet metastasized. In his mind that was really good news, but I was still in denial about even having cancer. Without a biopsy nobody knew for certain what was happening in my lung.

Since my chest discomfort was not heart related, Dr. Vargas passed me onto Dr. Kenneth Fuquay, a pulmonary specialist, with my first appointment scheduled later that afternoon. Of course, Dr. Fuquay previewed my MRI and PET scans and during that appointment scheduled me to take a 'breathing test.' Initially, I was amused because, of course, I know how to breathe. The test, however, proved to be more daunting than expected. Dr. Fuquay wanted that test to determine the breathing capacity of my lungs. They were excellent.

Next, he scheduled me to have a bronchoscopy, a biopsy for a lung, on Friday, March 12th as outpatient surgery at JMC. It's a tricky procedure since it involves going down the esophagus, bearing left at the fork in the bronchial tube and taking samples from the left lung. Once again, I was given anesthesia that put in la-la land. Dr. Fuquay would have the results at my next appointment on Wednesday, March 17th. Believe it or not, I still remained unconcerned about cancer.

Beware! If a doctor moves up an appointment, his patient usually has a severe problem. I took a telephone call from the doctor's office saying that he wanted to see me on Tuesday, March 16th instead of our scheduled appointment the next day. Failing to connect the dots, I blithely went to that appointment without concern.

Dr. Fuquay finally gave me the diagnosis I had avoided for weeks—I had a very large adenocarcinoma, a malignant tumor, growing in my left lung. *That was the greatest shock of my life!*

I'm a non-smoker, not that I would be immune from lung cancer, but it shocked me nevertheless. My brother smoked his entire life and cancer took him at 57, no surprise there. But I never smoked, adhering to conventional wisdom for maintaining a healthy lifestyle; it did no good.

My maternal grandfather was a coal miner who passed away at the ripe old age of 92. Think about that, a coal miner passing at 92! I figured I was bulletproof because of great genes.

The greatest shock was that less than ten months earlier I had back surgery in which several chest X-rays were taken which were normal. How could I be in such excellent health on May 21, 2009, and in less than ten months have an enormous tumor growing in my left lung threatening to kill me? Once again, my world was being turned upside down.

What caused this tumor? Dr. Fuquay thought radon poisoning while living up North may have been the culprit. While I considered his opinion a stretch, I had no better answer.

If any tumor or malignancy existed at all, however tiny and undetectable prior to back surgery, my immune system may have been compromised allowing unrestrained growth. That, too, seemed to be a stretch.

Also, considering the number of CT scans, MRIs and X-rays I had prior to back surgery, perhaps any one of them, either individually or collectively, may have triggered a malignancy in my lung.

While the cause remained unknown, that cancer needed be removed surgically.

Who would be my surgeon? The surgeons for my brain tumor, prostate cancer, and back surgery were at the top of their respective fields; they were the best. Dr. Fuquay scheduled an appointment for me with a Dr. Anderson, a thoracic surgeon, on March 18th, two days later. I knew nothing about him. Julie's boss, who's knowledgeable about many subjects, raved about a "Dr. Bob." At one time they were neighbors and she considered him the best thoracic surgeon in Florida.

Janet and I met Dr. Anderson at his office in Jupiter on that Thursday, and that's when we discovered Dr. Anderson's first name was Robert; *he was 'Dr. Bob!'* Hallelujah! Our paths just happened to cross at another critical intersection in my life. Thank you, Lord. He was not as intimidated about the position of the tumor as was Dr. Vargas, but told me that because of the size and location of the tumor, spanning both the upper and lower lobes in my lung that he may have to remove the entire lung to eliminate all cancer.

Our appointment was very businesslike and he concluded it by scheduling surgery one week later at the Jupiter Medical Center. Before leaving, however, Janet whispered to me to suggest to his office manager that I'd be willing to have surgery earlier, if possible, at any local hospital. I offered that suggestion to the office manager and we left.

About ten minutes later as we were driving home, I took a phone call from the office manager who said if I would be willing to have surgery at the Palm Beach Gardens Medical Center, I could have it done the very next day. Yes! Yes! Yes! Apparently, the office manager jumped on that suggestion, phoned the Gardens hospital and when told of an opening confirmed it with Dr. Anderson. Laura and Peter were both born at the Gardens Medical Center and that decision was a no-brainer for us. As I was driving home heading north, immediately, I turned our car around and headed south towards Palm Beach Gardens. Time to pre-register.

That massive adenocarcinoma growing in my lung had not yet metastasized as evidenced by the PET scan only ten days earlier. Dr. Anderson must have realized that with the size of the tumor with its potential to metastasize, an earlier surgery would benefit me. I wondered how much of his schedule Dr. Bob had to rearrange to accommodate my sudden surgery.

It took over two hours to pre-register at the Gardens Medical Center and after driving Janet home in the early afternoon, I went to a Jupiter medical facility for one final MRI.

By mid-afternoon I was done and returned home to be surprised by house guests—Pete and Linda Salzer, whom we enjoyed in the Hamptons exactly three months earlier, December 18th. They had flown down to attend a family wedding, but had time for a quick visit. What a blessing!

Pete's a surgeon himself and Linda a nurse, as well as a teacher, and they both encouraged me. Pete even checked up on Dr. Bob Anderson and gave his stamp of approval. Their timing was perfect—within 24 hours of my next major surgery.

Surgery was scheduled for 12:30 PM, Friday, March 19th. Naturally, Janet accompanied me to the hospital and Pastor Norman was there and prayed for me. The activity prior to surgery was a whirlwind, but once the anesthesia kicked in, I was out for the count.

I woke up many hours later in yet another recovery room and my first sensation was the soreness in my left arm and shoulder. The surgical team had to raise my left arm to remove the tumor for the duration of surgery, literally for hours.

Dr. Anderson made a five inch incision under my left pectoral muscle and removed an 11-centimeter malignant tumor—*the size of a grapefruit!*—along with my entire left lung. He ordered biopsies on 17 lymph nodes, and one was malignant but was contained within the lung that was removed. Surgery was successful. Of course, my left side was numb along with my left bronchial tube that Dr. Anderson needed to cut to remove the lung.

I quickly realized an ironic twist to this latest surgery. The enormous size of that tumor likely saved my life. Cancer is like a stealth bomber; it wants to remain hidden and does not announce its presence until "WHAM!"—it's too late. I was unaware of cancer, but literally *felt* something on the left side of my chest. It was that sensation that compelled me to see Dr. Vargas in the first place, setting in motion three weeks of intense drama.

People encouraged me by relating how John Wayne had a lung removed and lived well after surgery. I fully intended to live my life with gusto although somewhat dialed down. It should come as no surprise that lung cancer was *"my harrowing experience number nine!"*

There were some interesting parallels with my brain tumor in 1979, and the lung cancer in 2010. Within 24 hours before my brain tumor was even discovered, I was in a Benny Hinn service in which his fiancée, Suzanne, prayed healing for me. Within 24 hours of first meeting with Dr. Vargas, Janet and I had Pastor Norman and Judy Benz for dinner in our home and people in their church immediately began to pray healing for me once the mass was discovered in my lung.

The last headache I experienced with my brain tumor was on Friday, May 25, 1979, *exactly three weeks* before surgery on Friday, June 15, 1979. I first saw Dr. Vargas on Friday, February 26, 2010, and had surgery for lung cancer *exactly three weeks* later on Friday, March 19, 2010.

That brain tumor was identified as an astrocytoma, a deadly killer, but was surgically removed and I lived! That adenocarcinoma in my lung rapidly grew to the size of a grapefruit, but never metastasized and it, too, was surgically removed and once again, I lived!

In both cases I felt the Lord carried me through these most perilous times and experienced no fear. That's not even normal; that's grace.

Perhaps the most sobering fact about this ordeal was that a 62-year-old gentleman from our church was first diagnosed with lung cancer on June 2, 2010. Less than four weeks later, he died. Three weeks after seeing Dr. Vargas I had surgery to remove that massive cancerous tumor in my lung and lived. I have no pat answer for that. People in our church prayed for him as well as me and the Lord certainly didn't love him any less than He loved me. I have concluded the veracity of those words penned by David in Psalm 139:16:

> "Your eyes saw my substance, being yet unformed,
> And in Your book they all were written,
> The days fashioned for me,
> When as yet there were none of them."

My Father God, and Him alone, had established the number of days of my life, and quite simply, *my time is not up.*

After leaving the hospital I needed constant care and, once again, Janet used up all her sick/personal days. This time Peter, who lived in Ft. Worth, Texas and was in-between jobs, took a flight to care for me.

Janet and I had booked a cruise for spring break only weeks away, but guess who couldn't go—the one convalescing. Instead of Janet going with anybody else, we decided to purchase a third ticket and give our cruise vacation to Julie, Laura and Peter. This time Janet cared for me during her spring break while our adult children frolicked in the Caribbean.

44
COMPLICATIONS, CHEMOTHERAPY, AND HAWAII

D R. FUQUAY ASSIGNED me an oncologist, Dr. Edit Tolnai, who, coincidentally, had worked with the same group that treated my brother, George, twelve years earlier. She had just recently opened her own practice in Jupiter. Janet and I first met Dr. Tolnai during that whirlwind on the day of surgery and we were both comfortable with her. She got our attention by telling us cancer feeds on sugar. Guess who has a sweet tooth!

She mentioned having chemotherapy treatments after my chest was healed to knock out any residual cancer cells meandering through my body. I couldn't dispute that logic. George had gone through eight years of chemotherapy and although it was difficult, that treatment extended his life for years. Of course, after lung surgery, I expected to be cancer-free.

The medical team strongly encouraged me to take my medication to alleviate pain and promote healing; they didn't want the pain to 'get ahead of me.' Dutifully, I took the meds. However, people have differing biological make-ups and a medication that benefits one may not have the same effect on another.

After about two weeks of taking the meds, I began to feel nauseous and ultimately vomited. Vomiting is never pleasant, even when healthy, and this time I was convalescing after my lung was surgically removed and left bronchial tube cut and closed off. I vomited about four times in a two-week span and in the past usually felt better after vomiting. This time the nausea remained and I was discouraged; I didn't feel better.

Dr. Tolnai had done some blood work on me and was alarmed because my liver enzymes skyrocketed. What now? She immediately arranged for me to have another MRI of my digestive tract in which I had to drink an awful tasting liquid to enhance the images. I was already nauseous and drinking that thickened "goo" only made it worse; I couldn't finish it. Fortunately, I still had the MRI which revealed my liver was fine, but my gall bladder was problematic.

The meds, it had to be the meds. I spoke with my surgeon, Dr.

Anderson, and together we agreed to have me stop taking the pain meds. Unfortunately, my gall bladder had been affected.

Dr. Tolnai wanted no complications such as a potential gall bladder infection during chemotherapy; she said that could be harmful for my wellbeing. The gall bladder could have been treated with other medications, but that would have delayed chemotherapy indefinitely. Dr. Tolnai already needed to wait for my bronchial tube to be healed, but not a moment longer. The solution was surprisingly simple—remove my gall bladder. Suddenly, I was losing body parts at an alarming rate.

Surgery was scheduled for Friday, April 23rd, at the Jupiter Medical Center, exactly five weeks after lung cancer surgery. A local surgeon removed my gall bladder and I was released from the hospital a couple days later. I experienced no sickness after the gall bladder was removed which meant I was healthy enough to begin chemotherapy. I wasn't exactly leaping for joy since horror stories abound of chemotherapy. However, I appreciated Dr. Tolnai's reasoning as she was looking out for my best interests.

In pondering the events of the past year I found it remarkable that I had undergone five medical procedures all initiated with anesthesia. That was a personal record I never want to repeat. Starting off this unpleasant sequence was back surgery on May 21, 2009, then a colonoscopy in January, 2010 (since my dad had colon cancer), next came the bronchoscopy in mid-March followed closely by lung cancer surgery on March 19th and concluding with gall bladder surgery on April 23rd. That was a year to forget, and the paradox is that I still considered myself healthy.

Dr. Tolnai scheduled chemotherapy for four sessions, each being three weeks long. She knew we had planned vacations that summer, but insisted that I not travel during chemotherapy. Should I experience difficulties during chemo, I needed to be close to my doctors, not thousands of miles away.

Our personal travel agent, Julie, had arranged for us to vacation in Kauai, Hawaii, for nine days beginning June, 30th. Once again, Janet and I used frequent flyer miles to book our flight which we planned in the summer of 2009. Since I was ordered not to travel, our modified plan had Janet, Julie, and Laura enjoying Kauai while I remained homebound. Yuk! My niece, Lisa, would fly down from Massachusetts to care for my elderly mom, our dog, Max, and me. On consecutive summers I was being confined for medical reasons, but, still, was grateful to be alive and walking.

Janet and I also planned to attend another mini-reunion with Columbia teammates merely nine months after first connecting with them at that football game in New Hampshire. This time Bob Klingensmith arranged for a wine-tasting tour in Central California later that summer. There would have been be about 18 of us with our wives attending along with one of my fraternity brothers, who, coincidentally, connected with Bob at their gym. We booked this trip before knowing about lung cancer. Needless to say, I was disappointed to miss both vacations, but followed doctor's orders.

My first chemotherapy session occurred on Monday, May 10, 2010, in a cancer-patient building at the Jupiter Medical Center. I insisted on driving myself since I expected to be fine. I did not want to subject Janet or my daughters to watch those IVs dripping into me which would be as exciting as watching grass grow.

Prior to starting chemo, the nurse gave me a choice. Did I want a 'port' inserted one time into my body for all four sessions or have the staff stick me each time I went. Not wanting to be inconvenienced with a port in my body for nine weeks, I elected to be stuck those four times. At the first session, the nurse easily stuck that IV needle in my arm.

A new lung cancer drug—Alimta—was being used which did not cause hair loss. I appreciated that as I did not want to lose hair and expose to the world the scar on the top of my crown from brain surgery. My other chemo drug was Cisplatin, but before either of these 'heavy hitters' was given, I was hydrated with a saline solution for a couple hours. The first treatment took nearly six hours and afterwards I drove myself home that afternoon uneventfully.

The day after chemo, I returned to that cancer-patient building for a shot of Neulasta, a powerful drug to stimulate growth of new white blood cells. Apparently, chemotherapy drugs are indiscriminating in killing blood cells; they kill the white as well as well as the red. Then, I drove to Dr. Tolnai's office where a nurse drew a blood sample for analysis.

This was vital as it would reveal to Dr. Tolnai how my blood was reacting to the chemo drugs. I felt well.

My next session was scheduled for three weeks later, Monday, May 31st, but that happened to be Memorial Day, a national holiday. Instead, I had chemotherapy the next day, Tuesday, June 1st—our wedding anniversary. That was not the most romantic way to celebrate 42 years of marital bliss, but survival trumped romance. Janet still worked, I had my treatment and we quietly acknowledged our anniversary that evening.

One day later I got my shot of Neulasta and provided another blood sample for Dr. Tolnai. By Thursday her receptionist phoned me to say my blood work was "excellent."

That word changed everything.

Oddly enough, Julie never canceled my flight to Kauai. My family *really* enjoys vacationing together and knowing the clock was ticking down, Julie pleaded with me to ask Dr. Tolnai one more time if I could travel. When I asked Dr. Tolnai, she pondered my question before answering. Since I was handling the chemo well and my blood counts were excellent, she relented and said I could travel. Hawaii, here I come!

My third treatment was Tuesday, June 22nd, and by this time I recognized the pattern—the first week was typically unpleasant with the nausea, fatigue and having a metallic taste in my mouth, but those side effects gradually tapered off.

That treatment also became the most traumatic as several nurses stuck me about six times looking for a cooperative vein, but never found one. For somebody squeamish about being pricked with needles, I felt miserable. Facing failure, those nurses called for reinforcements - the 'pick' nurse from the hospital. She arrived, located a cooperative vein and poked me for the IV. Session three then proceeded uneventfully.

Most alarming about the chemo treatments was losing weight. I had dropped down to 178 and hadn't been that light since some time in high school. Merely one year earlier I had weighed 230 with an obvious jelly belly. I told Janet I felt like a 'stick' man; all my movements were herky-jerky, like the Frankenstein monster. She laughed.

Although Janet, Julie and Laura wanted to include me for our summer vacation, they also had concerns. Since I was undergoing chemotherapy with only one lung, would I be in danger breathing that recirculated air during the long flights between Florida and Kauai. My three amigos had the solution for me: wear a medical mask during those flights. I dreaded that thought, but understood their concern. In discussing this with Dr. Tolnai, she didn't think wearing a mask would be necessary unless there was actually a sick person coughing and wheezing on our flights. My family was not convinced.

Another concern was our lodging in Kauai, a three story walk-up with no elevator. Furthermore, our bedroom was in a loft above the main living level with yet another flight of stairs. How would I manage all those stairs with recent back surgery, atrophied calf muscles, one lung and chemo drugs flowing through me?

Furthermore, our apartment was not air-conditioned. In Florida that would be intolerable in June and July, but we're talking about Hawaii and not South Florida.

Finally, their idea of a vacation in paradise was one of constant activity (snorkeling, boating, shopping, sightseeing) while I only wanted to chill out while in the middle of chemotherapy. I was handling chemo well, but how would I handle Kauai?

As we began our adventure from Palm Beach International Airport, I *almost* got sick from the chemo drugs, having dry-heaves instead. I wore my mask on the flight both ways. It was ironic that a young mother with her newborn freaked out when she saw me wearing the mask and quietly asked Janet if I had some communicable disease. Janet replied by saying I had one lung and simply wanted to protect myself from her and everybody else breathing that re-circulated air in the cabin.

Walking up and down the stairways posed no problems, although I was slower than my energetic wife and daughters. The trade winds kept the temperatures comfortable, especially at night with low humidity and I was still able to do some passive sight-seeing.

All four of us enjoyed the Kilohana Plantation (where we took a train ride viewing the local flora and fauna), observed the Waimea Canyon (the largest in the USA besides the Grand Canyon), viewed the beginning of the Napali Coast from an elevation of 3,400 feet (where Jurassic Park was filmed), enjoyed lunch at the beautiful St. Regis Hotel (overlooking scenic Hanalei Bay), toured a botanical garden (with its variety of sculpted figurines), and saw Spouting Horn (a surprisingly loud, natural blow-hole).

Our most endearing experience, however, was meeting a friend of Janet's whom she had known since high school and college and had been a bridesmaid in our wedding. Janet hadn't seen Cindy since our wedding day, June 1, 1968, yet they recently connected on Facebook. She and her husband, Tony, were taking a cruise to the Hawaiian Islands and would be docking in Kauai at the exact time of our vacation.

Janet and I picked up Cindy and Tony at Kauai's port and greeted them warmly. We could have shown them more of Kauai's sites, but instead opted for a leisurely lunch and just shared the highlights of the past four decades. We all enjoyed reminiscing.

Upon returning to South Florida, I immediately contacted Dr. Tolnai to ask for one more favor. Since I was managing chemo well, my blood work remained excellent and had just returned from Hawaii without incident, would she allow me to travel to California for a mini-reunion with college teammates? She pondered my query longer than Hawaii because this time there was zero margin of error. My final chemo treatment would be Tuesday, July 13th, I would have the Neulasta shot and blood work the next day, the 14th, and our flight was departing the 15th. Nevertheless, she said I could go.

Earlier, I e-mailed Bob Klingensmith expressing my regrets about not being able to attend. He notified our teammates and commented that I was the Audie Murphy—the most decorated soldier in WWII—of our team because I had survived a brain tumor, prostate cancer, back surgery with a benign tumor, lung cancer and was currently undergoing chemotherapy. I was pleased to inform him that my oncologist changed her mind and cleared me to travel.

The mini-reunion was scheduled for Sunday, July 18th through Wednesday, July 21st in Solvang, east of Santa Barbara in Central California.

Before the reunion, however, Janet and I visited my fraternity brother and dear friend, Victor Obninsky, in Sonoma, California, north of San Francisco. Victor and I celebrated our graduation that night of June 1, 1966. Naturally, we reminisced about college days, shared our common Christian beliefs and commiserated over the loss of Russ Equi, a fraternity brother who became my best friend. He was killed in Vietnam.

45
MY BEST FRIEND RUSS

I'VE OFTEN TOLD my children that sometimes life isn't fair; Russ proved that. We first met on Columbia's freshman football team in September, 1962; we were both 'ends.' He pledged Phi Gamma Delta that fall while I waited until the spring to become a Fiji. It wasn't considered a 'jock' house since Russ and I were the only football players in the fraternity, although there were a couple basketball players, several wrestlers, and a bunch of guys from the crew teams, both lightweight and heavyweight.

Being both football players and fraternity brothers, we bonded. In May 1963, he and I saw the movie *Tom Jones* starring a young Albert Finney and Susannah York in a Times Square movie, and did we ever howl. He loved to laugh.

As sophomores we roomed together in our fraternity along with Larry Zuckerman in the least desirable room called 'the pit' because it was somewhat of a thorough-fare with several 'brothers' passing through our room to reach theirs. Being young and naive, we didn't care. I always found it interesting that Russ was Catholic, I was Protestant (Lutheran), and Larry was Jewish, yet we got along well. The three of us roomed together as juniors and seniors in a small apartment on W. 114th Street, just west of Broadway. Russ was a conscientious student who knew how to cram.

Football is controlled violence and not for the faint-hearted. Russ and I both played college football for four years and while I started all games my freshman year as a tight end and my varsity years as a tackle, he rode the bench. Yet, he participated in all the rigorous practices, including the preseason twice-a-day slug-fests at Camp Columbia, attended all team meetings and rode the bus 30 minutes each way between campus and Baker Field, but never played.

What motivated Russ?

He was pre-med and believed that having four years of college football would enhance his resume and help him get into medical school. He was focused and highly motivated.

Our final football game as seniors was against Brown at Baker Field.

They creamed us. Because we were getting clobbered early, the coaches inserted Russ to play defensive end in his final college football game. Russ became the only bright spot in an otherwise dismal performance. After the game I overheard one of our coaches mutter to himself about Russ, "Maybe we were the fools…" Although he weighed only 185 pounds, he played with enormous heart. That was Russ.

We lived only fifteen miles apart in Connecticut, and, no, we didn't face-off in high school football. After graduating from Columbia, however, we did hang out during summer break. Often, I drove to his house and met his mom, dad, and three sisters before seeing a movie, playing minia-ture golf, or, of all things, skateboarding. Give us a secluded incline—we didn't want to explain why two Ivy League grads would act like little kids out for a thrill—as we tested our skateboarding prowess. We weren't very good, but we had a blast and never wiped out.

We engaged in some lively discussions regarding the Vietnam War and who should actively fight the war and yes, we did talk religion, but we were best of friends, after all.

Russ's dream became reality as he was accepted into medical school. However, he was mischievous and told me that in his first year he and his med-school roommate threw a water balloon at another student and were nailed. The administration was not amused and expelled Russ with the explanation that medical students should be more mature than to engage in such pranks. Not surprisingly, that event changed Russ's life.

Knowing that he would likely be drafted into the army and sent to Vietnam, Russ signed up to become a Marine officer. However, before reporting for assignment, he visited me in Pittsburgh in May 1968, wearing his Marine uniform and I was pleased to introduce him to my betrothed merely weeks before our wedding. He approved. Janet phoned her friend, Cindy, to join us for a blind date with Russ that evening.

At the end of the evening I gave Russ my car keys to drive Cindy to her dorm, but they never made it. He slammed into another car with both of them catapulting into the windshield as they were not wearing seat belts. Although they were bloodied, neither was seriously injured although both cars were totaled. Janet and I have buckled up ever since.

Russ and I corresponded a little, but that ended abruptly when Mom phoned me in early 1969, to tell me that Russ, my best friend, was just killed in Vietnam. I was devastated and bawled. In my last letter to Russ, I made a typical college-kid, smart-alec remark, "Don't step on anything!"

I have since learned that while on a mission to clear a minefield, his AMTRAC discharged an explosive that detonated prematurely and he was blown up instantly along with his crew. He had only weeks to complete his tour of duty in Vietnam.

My son, Peter, visited Washington, D.C. when he was in sixth grade and went to the Vietnam Memorial where he made a rubbing of Russell's name to give to me. I never contacted his parents or sisters afterwards because I didn't know what to say. I do now.

One thought comforts me. He and I talked about life after death and heaven and I fully expect that when I pass to the other side, I'll be greeted by my best friend, Russ. We are eternal beings.

46
VACATIONS, PART 2

JANET AND I enjoyed Victor's hospitality for several days before driving south to our motel in Solvang.

It was great to renew friendships after 44 years. Of course, some of those attending we had seen only nine months earlier at the Columbia-Dartmouth game. I particularly enjoyed seeing our team captain, Ron Brookshire, who lived in California, and Lloyd Loomis, the fraternity brother who befriended Klinger at their gym. Once again, Bob did a masterful job organizing our itinerary and providing T-shirts to commemorate our "Sideways" reunion.

On Sunday evening we gathered at a lodge with a fabulous panoramic view of a valley below with mountains beyond for our first meal of pasta and wine. I abstained from wine. Before the meal I got sick since my last chemo treatment was only five days earlier and Janet and Bob comforted me. Dinner was fun and was capped off, once again, by singing that familiar fight song with gusto, "Roar, Lion, Roar."

During the next couple days we had tours of several wineries in Central California and I became the designated driver, when necessary.

At the reunion I expected to share my lung cancer story with the group and how, by the grace of God, it had never metastasized and I survived, but it never worked out. Instead, I spoke privately with each and every one of my teammates about my experience. Apparently, God had a better plan.

By Wednesday morning just about everybody had checked out or was leaving the motel. Janet and I bid our farewells as we, too, began our drive north to San Francisco for our return flight home. Janet wanted to travel north on California 1, the Big Sur road, to enjoy the scenery. I had driven Big Sur two times earlier and wasn't comfortable driving south since only a few feet away from the edge of the road was a perilous drop to the Pacific Ocean hundreds of feet below. Without guard rails in many locations, that ride unnerved me. However, we were heading north this time on the opposite side of the road; how bad could that be?

I soon found out. As we continued north the terrain became very mountainous. The road was winding, hugging the side of those mountains, steadily rising higher and higher above the Pacific Ocean. I literally couldn't take my eyes off the road for a second for fear of missing a turn and dared not to look at that breathtaking view of the Pacific hundreds of feet below. Later, Janet confessed to me she was hoping I wouldn't ask her to drive since she, too, was unnerved. We completed our trip safely although it seemed to take forever, but I never want to drive Big Sur again.

Our return flight from San Francisco to Miami was routine.

By now Janet was approaching the end of her summer vacation as I was nearing the end of chemotherapy. She, too, had suffered emotionally while caring for me since March and wanted to do something special. While on the Internet looking at recipes, Janet saw an advertisement pop up for Caribbean cruises and immediately phoned for information. There was one room available during the only week we could go and, not surprisingly, we booked it. It was a seven day Western Caribbean cruise to two countries we hadn't visited, Costa Rica and Panama.

Janet and I scheduled no shore excursions, but in Panama, we shared a cab with a father and his adult son to view the Canal. Since all of us were curious to see a ship actually traverse the locks, we had to wait for about an hour.

During that time I quietly chatted with the father about my recent lung cancer surgery and other experiences with God. He was not a believer and rejected everything I said, explaining in very natural terms what I had experienced supernaturally. He finally became belligerent about Jesus Christ and cursed Him. This grieved me, but I realized the truth of I Corinthians 2:14: *"... the natural man does not receive the things from the Spirit of God, they are foolishness to him ... "* (NKJV).

Still, Janet and I were blessed to be fully engaged as *"ambassadors for Christ"* (2 Corinthians 5:20).

Chemotherapy was now history, and Dr. Tolnai scheduled a PET scan for me on September 21, 2010. Was I cancer-free or not? I endured chemotherapy quite well and actually began to gain weight once again; the cruise definitely helped. Janet was pleased that my belly was finally flat, but I hardly recommend losing weight by having three surgeries topped off with chemotherapy in a little more than a year.

Finally, September 21st arrived and I had the PET scan. Once again, the most difficult part was finding a good vein. Initially, all efforts failed. Desperately, the nurse then tried three different locations on my hands before finally succeeding. I felt miserable, but thought of Jesus Christ having nails driven through his wrists and legs. Since He did that for me, surely I could tolerate a few more pin pricks through my own flesh. The scan itself was the easy part (as long as a person doesn't suffer from claustrophobia) and was completed in thirty minutes. In one week I had an appointment with Dr. Tolnai to review the results.

That day arrived. Of course, I had blood drawn, but the nurse had no problem since drawing blood apparently is so much easier than pumping something into me. Finally, I met Dr. Tolnai. We chatted briefly before she said the most beautiful words I would ever hear: *"Your scan was clear!" I AM CANCER-FREE!* That grapefruit-sized malignant tumor threatening to kill me was gone and left behind no rogue cancer cells.

Thank You, Lord, for granting me another day of life.

POSTSCRIPT

I T's GOOD TO be alive!

Although life did not turn out the way I expected, God consistently intervened and has blessed me beyond expectations. The Father introduced me to His Son, Jesus Christ, who became Lord of my life, I married my "ideal" woman and am still smitten by her, our three adult children know the Lord as we remain a close-knit family, Janet and I live in the home I designed and built while unemployed and still delight in it, and we've traveled extensively while on a limited budget…all by the grace of God.

Yet, our lives have not been easy.

While Janet still represents my "ideal" woman, "…tall, blond with blue eyes, well-endowed, long legs, shapely, and attractive," she was also wounded by sexual abuse, which has profoundly affected our marriage.

By nature, I am reserved and resolute, similar to my mother. She worked for the government for 30 years and that would be me—working for a company throughout my career before retiring. That never happened. Instead, I've been laid off twice as an architect and became self-employed for over 27 years in South Florida. Furthermore, I never considered becoming a general contractor, but, apparently, God did and even provided the name— Creative Custom Designs.

Conversely, Janet is outgoing and vivacious who thrives on interacting with people. Sadly, she never fulfilled her heart's desire to be that stay-at-home mom raising our children, but became a teacher virtually her entire adult life. During the 39 years of Janet's career, she developed discipline at The King's Academy and honed her teaching skills to become that master teacher no one could have foreseen, except, the Lord Himself. Her students were blessed and she was fulfilled.

In hindsight, God turned both Janet and me upside-down. I have become that man of faith by believing God and taking chances that my conservative temperament would never have allowed while Janet has become in the words of her principal at TKA, "the stability of third grade." Only the Lord could have transformed each of us so radically.

Also, I have come to realize that my first year architectural design instructor at Carnegie-Mellon was right. Architects don't necessarily make a ton of money! Yet, I enjoy the challenges of being an architect.

January 4, 1991, the day I was laid off from DiVosta, has become a pivotal day in my career. Prior to that date, every job I had...at Carl G. Baker & Associates, The Lawrence Group, Architects, the years at Crystal Tree and with DiVosta & Company, I worked in an office outside the home. After that day, I became self-employed and worked exclusively in my home office (with the exception of a three month stint as a consultant with another architect in West Palm Beach). One of the ironies of life is that if I never had been laid off from DiVosta, I would never have built our home.

I have heard that the Bible states 365 times to "fear not!" When facing life-threatening surgeries four times—brain surgery, prostate cancer, back surgery and lung cancer, I experienced no fear. Is that even normal? It was the Lord who carried me through those perilous times and He filled me with peace.

Aside from saving my life nine times, which in itself is mind-boggling, God did much more. While we weren't even seeking employment, He provided a good job for each person in our family, with Janet topping the list with three. While self-employed (the next step up from being unemployed), He enabled me to secure a construction loan to build a home in a gated community with 24/7 security...I've never met anyone who did that. After a 1200-mile road trip, He had Janet and me comfort Nana when Papa dropped dead of a heart attack merely hours after our arrival. Finally, the Lord provided $200,000 (tax-free) for the family that was prophesied to us nearly seven years earlier. God has been very real to me and my family as we have experienced His miracles as well as His presence day by day.

When that first neurosurgon called me a "walking time-bomb" on June 6, 1979, I have since come to realize that everybody alive is virtually a "walking time-bomb" as well. Why? Because nobody knows which day will be his or her last. Through accidents, illnesses, even murder, there's no guarantee that any one of us will live beyond this very day. I regard each day of life as a gift of God, and my responsibility is to be that "ambassador for Christ" during the time given to me. I am only one heartbeat away from eternity...and so are you!

ABOUT THE AUTHOR

JOHN M. NOSSAL is an architect and general contractor. He has degrees from Columbia and Carnegie-Mellon and moved to the Palm Beach area in 1972, to work as an architect. He is married to Janet, a teacher, and they have three children.

As a Lutheran in 1976, he attended a Cursillo (a Christian leaders weekend) in Miami, and had a born again experience. Janet soon followed and their lives have changed dramatically.

In the spring of 1979, John was diagnosed with a brain tumor and had surgery at the Columbia-Presbyterian Hospital in New York City. After being laid off in 1983, within a year he opened his own practice as an architect. In 1986, John took a phone call from Buz DiVosta, the largest developer in the area, whom he had never met, and months later became his Chief Architect. He was laid off again in 1991.

Motivated by a prophetic word, in 1992 John designed and built their home in a gated community in Tequesta, Florida.

Although John remains healthy, he has had several major surgeries, two to eliminate cancer along with back surgery and five potentially lethal accidents. He thanks God to be alive.

CONTACT THE AUTHOR

You may contact the author by visiting:

http://www.johnnossal.com.

John Nossal was the tallest one on his Little League team, 1957.

A two-year-old John Nossal with Dad and five-year-old brother, George, at picnic.

A nineteen-year-old John Nossal with Dad and brother, George, at beach..

The only play in eight years of football in which John's helmet was knocked off while the action continued, October 1964. *Sports Illustrated* was preparing a feature on Columbia's quarterback, Archie Roberts, a pre-season All American candidate in 1964, but John was featured in this pohto instead. The photographer is unknown.

John and Janet's wedding day picture, June 1, 1968, with proud parents

John Janet, Julie and Laura in 1890's attire, early December, 1978. The outfits were fake, but John's beard was real

John convalescing in hospital after brain surgery sporting a skull cap with a pleased Janet at his side.

Prisoners and team members of Raiford Cursillo #4. December, 1978. Jack Murphy is the tenth person from left in the back row with aviator sunglasses while John is centered in the back row in front of the larger bush.

The Nossal Family Home (since 1993) designed by John and built by John with men in the church.

Moments after John being rescured from nearly drowning in the Chattahoochi
River rapids with Peter, Laura, Janet and Julie, July 20, 1995

John and Janet on Alaskan glacier during 30th anniversary cruise, May, 1998

Nossal family in Tiki-hut during shore excursion of Caribbean cruise, January, 2005

John, Janet, Julie and Laura at Parthenon in Athens, Greece, summer, 2006, immediately before discovering prostate cancer

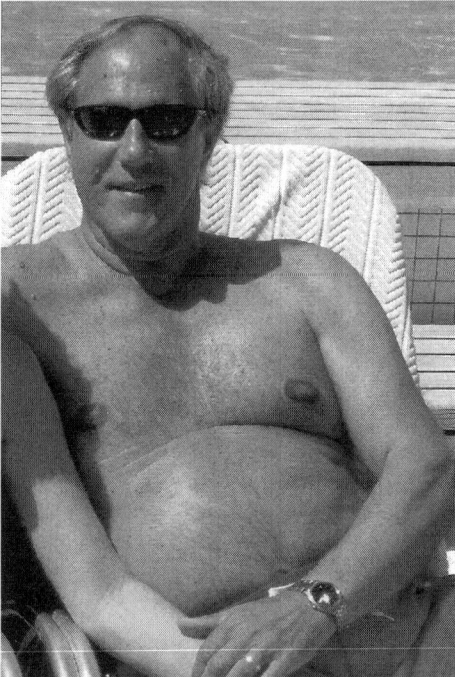

John weighing over 230 on Baltic cruise, summer, 2008

Columbia teammates and friends before boarding bus to
Columbia-Dartmouth football game, October, 2009.
First row: Barry Nazarian, Bob Klingensmith, Chuck Christenson;
second row: Rich Beggs, John Nossal, Dean Mottard, Tom Harold;
third row: Tom Chorba, Steve Franke, Bill Hiney, Gene Thompson, Earl werner;
last row: unknown person & Pete Salzar

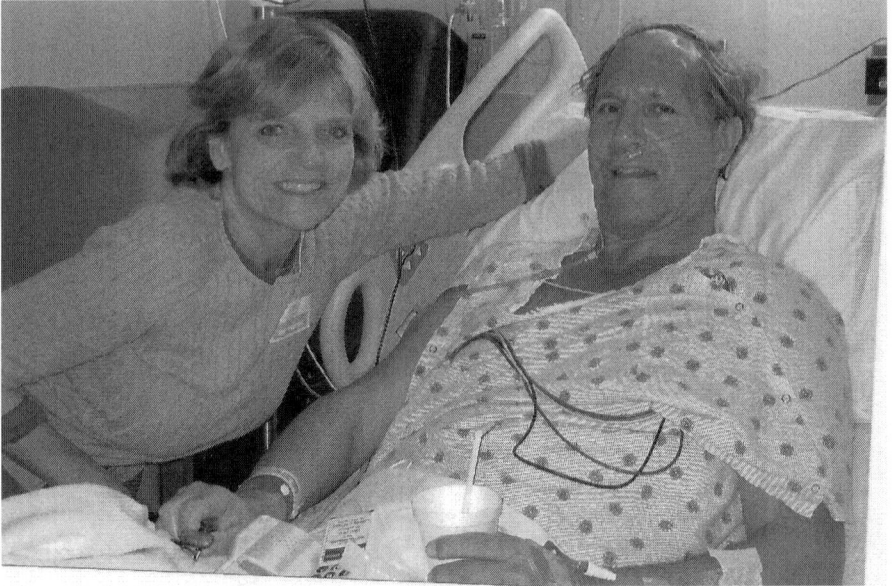

Glad to be alive after radical pulmonechtomy to eliminate lung cancer with Janet, March, 2010

My best friend, Russ Equi, killed in Vietnam, January, 1969. Photo was taken by Victor Obninsky in mid-1960's.

A thin John during chemotherapy along with Janet, Laura and
Julie while vacationing in Kauia, June, 2010.

John and Janet (seated) with Melissa, Peter, Laura and Julie
enjoying Butchart Gardens, Victoria, B.C., July, 2012

Made in the USA
Middletown, DE
15 November 2015